Simple Sermons on the Second Coming

Simple Sermons on the Second Coming

W. Herschel Ford

BAKER BOOK HOUSE
Grand Rapids, Michigan 49516

Copyright 1945 by Zondervan Publishing House
Grand Rapids, Michigan

Reprinted 1988 by Baker Book House
Grand Rapids, Michigan
with the permission of the copyright holder

ISBN: 0-8010-3542-2

Second printing, July 1989

Printed in the United States of America

DEDICATION

To my heart's closest and dearest friend
JAMES LEROY STEELE
*great Gospel preacher, true servant
of God, faithful comrade of the
years, I lovingly and cheerfully
dedicate this book in the
Name of Him whose
"appearing" we
both love*

INTRODUCTION

The "blessed hope" is a theme of perennial interest to all God's faithful children, and as our age advances into the inevitable darkness of its consummation we see that Christ's coming is also the world's only hope.

Any book, therefore, which deals Biblically and progressively with the tremendous event of the Second Advent will bless, instruct and prepare its readers for that ever-imminent event.

These pages reveal that Dr. Ford is a clear and forceful preacher of prophetic truth. His messages are plainly outlined, amply documented by Scripture quotations and illumined by illustration.

The author's progressive treatment of the theme is admirable. Beginning with the Rapture, he takes his readers through every major phase of both Rapture and Revelation to the grand consummation of a "new heaven and a new earth."

As we read these pages and note their solidness and sanity, we wish we might have heard the messages in their pulpit delivery. There is fire enough left in the printed word to tell of the blaze that their preaching must have kindled in the hearts of the author's listeners.

We believe also that the book will kindle wisps of spiritual flame wherever it goes—perhaps will help start the needed conflagration of a Holy Ghost Revival which may complete the "out-calling" of the Church in preparation for His "glorious appearing."

WILLIAM WARD AYER

New York, N. Y.

CONTENTS

1. WHAT WILL HAPPEN WHEN JESUS COMES IN THE AIR?....11
2. WHAT WILL HAPPEN IN HEAVEN AFTER JESUS COMES IN THE AIR?....................................22
3. WHAT WILL HAPPEN ON EARTH WHEN THE CHURCH IS GONE? 35
4. WHAT WILL HAPPEN WHEN JESUS RETURNS TO THE EARTH IN GLORY?................................50
5. WHAT WILL HAPPEN DURING THE MILLENNIUM?.........64
6. WHAT WILL HAPPEN AT THE GREAT WHITE THRONE?.....77
7. WHAT WILL HAPPEN WHEN THE WORLD IS NO MORE?....89

1

WHAT WILL HAPPEN WHEN JESUS RETURNS IN THE AIR?

> But I would not have you to be ignorant, brethren, concerning them which are asleep, that ye sorrow not, even as others which have no hope. For if we believe that Jesus died and rose again, even so them also which sleep in Jesus will God bring with him. For this we say unto you by the word of the Lord, that we which are alive and remain unto the coming of the Lord shall not prevent them which are asleep. For the Lord himself shall descend from heaven with a shout, with the voice of the archangel, and with the trump of God: and the dead in Christ shall rise first: then we which are alive and remain shall be caught up together with them in the clouds, to meet the Lord in the air: and so shall we ever be with the Lord. Wherefore comfort one another with these words (I Thessalonians 4:13-18).

SOME TIME ago I asked another preacher this question: "Do you preach on the Second Coming of Christ?" He replied, "No, I don't, but I notice that you have a house full of people when you preach on that subject." Why will not preachers preach on the Second Coming? This great truth certainly fills a large part of the Bible and the man who fails to preach on the Second Coming is neglecting a great portion of God's Word. A sermon on the Lord's return gives out definite Bible information, brings comfort and hope to God's people and furnishes a great incentive for service and right living. If we know that Jesus may come at any minute, and that we must meet Him face to face, surely every Christian should say, "I must be a better Christian and live a better life for my Lord." Now, why do crowds come when the preacher speaks on the Second Coming? They come because they are hungry for this Bible truth. They are living in a troubled world and they love to hear of One who is coming to deliver them from it all . . . of One who will conquer the forces of evil and will take His own to glory.

There was a time when I did not preach on the Lord's Second Coming. I did not think that this truth was plain enough nor important enough. I said to myself, "I know that He is coming, and that men ought to get ready for His coming." I still say that, but it is a blessed thing to go deeper than this into the doctrine of the Second Coming. The study of this doctrine has brought great blessing and comfort to my heart. It has explained many Scriptures which otherwise were not clear. I am afraid that many preachers omit the doctrine of the Second Coming, even when they are speaking on very familiar passages of Scripture. For instance, think of II Timothy 4:7-8:

> I have fought a good fight, I have finished my course, I have kept the faith: henceforth there is laid up for me a crown of righteousness, which the Lord, the righteous judge, shall give me at that day: and not to me only, but unto all them also that love his appearing.

We hear many sermons on these farewell words of Paul, but seldom do we hear the last phrase mentioned in these sermons: namely, these words, "but unto all them also that love his appearing." If we seek for Scriptures on the Second Coming we find them literally jumping out at us from almost every chapter in the New Testament.

I am grateful to those who have inspired me to make a more definite study of the Lord's return. I cannot point to the time nor to the teacher, but many circumstances have combined to cause me to study the doctrine and gradually

Simple Sermons on the Second Coming

the great truth was unfolded to my heart. Jesus said that the Holy Spirit would guide us into all truth. He is the great Interpreter of Bible truths, and I can humbly say that the Holy Spirit guided me and showed me these things.

I once had the old conception of a general judgment . . . a conception which is common to many people today. This idea is that Christ will come, gather all people before Him, pass judgment upon them and send them either to the right or the left . . . either to heaven or hell. If that conception is true, then man is not saved here, but he is saved or condemned out there somewhere in the future. Briefly I believe this to be the true conception: Christ will come in the air and take up all believers to be with Him. Later He will come back with them in great glory and He and His followers will reign a thousand years upon the earth. He then defeats all His enemies, casts Satan and his followers into the lake of fire, and leads His own people into eternal bliss. This conception clears up every question as to what will happen to the various people of the earth. The general judgment conception leaves a hundred questions unanswered.

Today Christ is in heaven with the Father, and the Holy Spirit is at work here on the earth. There are two groups of people in the world . . . the saved and the lost. There are no in-betweens. What will be the next thing to happen in the great prophetic drama? According to the Scriptures it will be the coming of Jesus in the air. Let us notice some facts about this coming.

I. THE GREAT SOUNDS

In I Thessalonians 4:16 we read:

> For the Lord himself shall descend from heaven with a shout, with the voice of the archangel, and with the trump of God.

1. *The shout.* This is the victor's shout. When Jesus comes He comes as a victor and there will be mighty power

in His shout. It will penetrate all the graves, pierce to the deepest depths of the sea and will be heard by every saint upon the earth. We once thought that such a thing was impossible, but now the miracle of radio teaches us that one voice can be heard all over the world. If God gave us the radio, He can send the shout of His Son's voice into every corner of the universe.

Jesus went one day to the grave of Lazarus and cried out, "Lazarus, come forth"! Lazarus was dead, but he heard his Master's voice and came out of the grave. So it is that all His people who sleep in the earth or in the depths of the sea will hear His voice and come forth to meet Him. This shall be the redemption of the body. It may be that His shout will consist of just one word, and surely that word will be "Come." This is the royal word of grace . . . this is God's favorite word. He is saying now to lost men everywhere, "Come and be saved." In that day He will say to all who have believed on Him, "Come up with Me . . . come from the land and the air and the sea and the grave . . . come up to be with Me forever."

2. *The voice of the archangel.* The archangel is the leader of the heavenly hosts . . . he is directly connected with the descent of Jesus from heaven. There will be a great commotion in heaven when Jesus goes out, for He will be going out to get all the redeemed souls who have been saved by His grace. Yes, He will go out to bring them with their glorified bodies into the Father's house.

3. *The trump of God.* This shout stands for a great gathering together. When the trumpet blows in the army camp, the men rush from their tents and fall into line and march off to battle. When God's trump shall sound every saved person everywhere will fall in line and be taken up to join the great multitude of heaven. And the shout will be so loud and the voice will be so clear and the trump

will be so distinct that every child of God will hear and go up to meet Him.

II. THE GREAT SAVIOUR'S APPEARANCE

"The Lord himself shall descend." There will be no substitute. This One who comes is none other than the Lord Jesus Christ. This reminds us of what the men in white said to the disciples on the Mount of Olives as given in Acts 1:11:

> Ye men of Galilee, why stand ye gazing up into heaven? this same Jesus, which is taken up from you into heaven, shall so come in like manner as ye have seen him go into heaven.

It also reminds us of what Jesus said to the disciples in John 14:3:

> And if I go and prepare a place for you, I will come again, and receive you unto myself; that where I am, there ye may be also.

You may ask this question, "On what will Jesus stand at that time?" We say to you that He needs nothing on which to stand. He suspended the earth on nothing, did He not? He hung out the sun, which is thousands of times larger than the earth . . . He put the moon and the stars and the planets in the heavens. If He can do all that, I know that He can stay for a time in the air without visible support. Yes, the heavens will burst open and Jesus will come forth in all of His beauty. He will shout as He descends . . . the voice of the archangel will be heard . . . the trump of God will sound and yonder between the heavens and the earth the Saviour will hover, ready and waiting to snatch His children up out of this sinful world and take them home with Him.

Once before, Jesus was suspended between heaven and earth. Cruel men did it . . . they hung Him upon a Cross as if He were too good for earth and yet not good enough for heaven. That was a Cross of suffering, but, thank God, there will be no suffering for Him when He comes back. He will hover there between heaven and earth in beauty and majesty. His heart will be overflowing with anticipation, for soon He will meet His bride and take her home with Him. His anticipation was great when He hung upon the Cross, for in His heart He cried out, "Look unto me all ye ends of the earth and be ye saved!" He looked down through all the ages and saw those who would believe in Him. He knew the joy that would be in their hearts . . . He knew from what they would be saved and to what they would be saved. As He thought of all this He rejoiced in the privilege of making the supreme sacrifice to save lost men.

But now as He comes in the air His anticipation is greater. He is going to gather His believers from all over the earth. He is going to raise the bodies of all those who loved Him and died in the faith. This will be the greatest reunion the world has ever known. Every trouble will be over and Jesus will throw His loving arms around His believers and His own great heart will overflow with wondrous joy.

III. WHAT WILL HAPPEN TO THOSE ON THE EARTH WHEN HE COMES?

I will try to give you these events in Biblical order.

1. *The dead in Christ shall rise first.* When the trumpet sounds the dead believers will rise. Not every grave will be opened for those who died without Christ shall still sleep in their graves. We read these words: "Blessed and holy is he that hath part in the first resurrection." Those who die out of Christ are not blessed and holy . . . they must stay in their graves for another thousand years. Then after the tribulation period and after the millennium they will be raised and brought in judgment before the Great White Throne where they shall receive the condemnation of hell.

"Blessed are the dead which die in the Lord." These are

not lost . . . they are sleeping until He comes and then He will raise them up to be with Him. This is the reason Christians are not to mourn like others who have no hope. We know that when Jesus comes our saved loved ones who have tasted death will be the first ones to rise up to meet Him.

There are sleeping Christians in many different places of the earth. The majority of them are in man-made graves. However, many Christians have gone down into the seas . . . many have been burned to death . . . some have been lost in the wild places of the earth, and their bones have been picked clean by the birds of the air . . . some have suffered and died in the deserts and their bones have been left to bleach in the broiling sun . . . some have been torn to pieces in explosions . . . some have flown away in airplanes and have never been found. None of this matters to Jesus for He knows everything. He knows where they are and He will show forth His power over death when He comes, for His loved ones will rise from everywhere and not one of them shall be lost.

When I attend the funeral of a Christian I can truly say to him, "Good-bye, I will see you with Jesus after a little while." We can say this of all those who know Jesus for we know that it is well with them. Now, when the dead are taken up this is the first resurrection . . . it is not a resurrection of the dead but a resurrection from among the dead. The lost dead will be left in their graves, but the saved ones will be raised incorruptible.

2. *The living Christians will then be caught up.* Every Christian on the earth will hear His commanding shout and will rise up to meet Him. It may be that an engineer will be taken from a moving train . . . a pilot from his speeding plane . . . the operator of an electric plant from his dynamos. Then the worldlings who are left will surely know the value that a Christian is to the world.

Will every Christian in the world be caught up? Yes, every one. Some people say that only those who have a certain spiritual experience or have reached a certain depth of consecration will be caught up. Some say that only those who have a correct knowledge of the Second Coming will be caught up. Some even go so far as to say that those who cannot talk in tongues will not be caught up. All of these are wrong . . . the Scripture nowhere teaches anything about a partial Rapture.

The basis of salvation and rapture is not that of works, but of faith in Christ. If you have believed in Him and trusted in Him . . . if you have been born again . . . you will go to meet Him. I am not saying that every church member will be caught up, but I am saying that every true child of God will have a part in the Rapture. And the greater his faithfulness, the greater shall be his joy and reward in that day.

Suppose that a man was saved at nine o'clock and that Jesus came in the air at ten o'clock. This man would not have time to learn much about Christ or read his Bible or grow in grace, yet he would be caught up just as would the best saint living on the face of the earth. Suppose that you were saved on Sunday night and the Lord's return was on Monday before you were baptized . . . you would be caught up just the same because our salvation is based on faith and not on baptism.

The thief yonder on the cross cried out, "Lord, remember me when thou comest into thy kingdom," and Jesus said to him, "Verily I say unto thee, To day shalt thou be with me in paradise." The dying thief's soul went to be with the Lord, and, although he had no time to do anything for Christ, his body will be raised along with that of Stephen and Paul when Jesus comes in the air. As all dead Christians shall be raised up at His coming, so shall all living Christians be caught up to meet Him in the air.

We often sing the familiar words, "He will give me grace

and glory." He gives the grace now, and we shall have the glory then. In the eighth chapter of Romans we are told that He justifies and glorifies. He justifies us now because of our faith in Him . . . we will be glorified then when we go up to meet Him.

Jesus is the head of the Church and we are the body. At His coming body and head will be joined. If some of us were left on the earth the body would not be complete, and it is His purpose to raise a complete body. We read in Romans 14:10 that all of us must "stand before the judgment seat of Christ." We shall stand there, not to receive condemnation, but a reward. If all of us are to stand before Him in that day, all of us must be taken up out of the earth. Therefore, all Christians, whether dead or alive, will be taken up to meet Jesus in the air.

3. *Another great event will also occur.* A wondrous change will come both for the dead and living saints. We read in I Corinthians 15:51-53:

> Behold, I shew you a mystery; We shall not all sleep, but we shall all be changed, in a moment, in the twinkling of an eye, at the last trump: for the trumpet shall sound, and the dead shall be raised incorruptible, and we shall be changed. For this corruptible must put on incorruption, and this mortal must put on immortality.

Here we are definitely told that the dead saints shall be raised incorruptible and that the living saints shall all be changed.

When we meet Jesus in the air our bodies will be changed. We shall be like Him . . . sinless and perfect. We do not know just what kind of body this will be. Paul calls it a "spiritual body," but surely it is enough for us to know that we shall be like Jesus at the end of the way. We want to be like Him here, but we are hindered by our sin and the desires of the flesh. However, in that minute when He comes we will be free from all evil and we will not be ashamed to meet Him for we will be like Him.

How long will it take God to change our bodies and make us like Jesus? He will bring about this marvelous transformation "in the twinkling of an eye." God knows how to do things instantaneously. He said, "Let there be light," and light was diffused over the whole world. He can save a person the minute that person believes in Christ. I believe in instantaneous conversion. We are not forced to wait a lifetime and then have the good and the bad evaluated before a decision is made about our salvation. We are saved forever the second we believe, and so it is that the very second Jesus comes in the air the greatest change in the world will come to you and me. We will drop this old sinful flesh and be made like unto Him.

Yes, Jesus will come in the air, the dead will be raised incorruptible, the living saints will be changed and made like Him, and then we shall all be caught up to meet Him in the air.

Now this expression "caught up" suggests an eagle catching up his prey and carrying it off toward the mountain peak. It suggests a strong man rescuing a child from the path of a truck and dashing off with that child to safety. Yes, the Church will be snatched away before the Great Tribulation overtakes a godless world. The unsaved will be left on earth to go through that awful period.

All of us are air-minded today. Thousands of planes are flying around the world, carrying tens of thousands of men. These mighty machines must rise on the power of their own motors, but when Jesus comes we will rise through the magnetic power of Him who draws all men unto Himself. Some people are afraid to go up into the air today, but in that day we shall have no fear. We shall be like Jesus and all fear will be cast out. We shall be looking up, listening to Him, moving toward Him and enjoying that matchless moment of meeting Him in the air.

Now what will happen to the saints after they are caught up to meet Jesus in the air? That will be told in the next chapter. I shall close this chapter with this thought: We do not know when He is coming and so it is our responsibility to get ready. Surely, we all want to be among those whom He will change and take up with Him. May God pity those who are left to stand before the Great White Throne!

John, the beloved, stood yonder on the Isle of Patmos. The lonely old man longed for the sight of the best Friend he had ever had. He wanted to drop off his robe of flesh and go up to meet his Saviour. I can see him as he looks into the sky and I can hear him, his voice breaking a little as he cries out, "Even so, come, [quickly], Lord Jesus!" Can you say that today, or do you shrink at the thought of His coming?

A Christian man lay dying. He had three sons, two of whom were Christians, but the third and youngest was a wayward sinner. The old man spoke to the two boys who were Christians and said: "I am going to leave you for a little while, but it won't be for long. I will see you again some day . . . good-night." But to the youngest son he said, "Good-bye, my son, good-bye." And this boy, with a breaking heart, cried out, "Father, why do you say good-bye to me with such finality and tell my brothers that you will see them before long?" The old man replied, "Your brothers trust my Saviour as their Saviour. You have rejected Him and those who do this never find the way to the heavenly home . . . this is the parting of the way for us forever." The poor boy broke down and sobbed and said, "Oh, Father, just tell me good-night for a little while . . . I, too, trust the Saviour right now . . . I will see you again some day."

How is it going to be with you? Do you know Jesus? Are you ready for His coming? When He does come will you be one of His own?

2

WHAT WILL HAPPEN IN HEAVEN AFTER JESUS COMES IN THE AIR?

Let a man so account of us, as of the ministers of Christ, and stewards of the mysteries of God. Moreover it is required in stewards, that a man be found faithful. But with me it is a very small thing that I should be judged of you, or of man's judgment: yea, I judge not mine own self. For I know nothing by myself; yet am I not hereby justified: but he that judgeth me is the Lord. Therefore judge nothing before the time, until the Lord come, who both will bring to light the hidden things of darkness, and will make manifest the counsels of the hearts: and then shall every man have praise of God (I Corinthians 4:1-5).

Wherefore we labour, that, whether present or absent, we may be accepted of him. For we must all appear before the judgment seat of Christ; that every one may receive the things done in his body, according to that he hath done, whether it be good or bad (II Corinthians 5:9-10).

SOMEONE MAY say to me, "How do you know what is going to happen in the future? You are not a prophet and you cannot see into the dim unknown." If so, I will answer by saying, "I am not going to tell you what I think, but I am going to look into the Bible and tell you what I find there. I know that these things are going to happen because God says so in His Book." The trouble with many people is that they interpret events in their own hearts and minds instead of looking into the Bible.

Each week we mail from our church a bulletin containing the church news and the announcements for the coming

Sunday. This bulletin has a heading which says, *Dr. Ford's Sermon Subjects for Sunday.* Under this heading are given both the morning and the evening sermon topics. This bulletin reaches our members on Friday. Suppose that one of them said to someone on Saturday, "Dr. Ford is going to preach tomorrow on such-and-such a subject." Then the question would be asked, "How do you know?" and the answer would be given, "These subjects have been announced in the church bulletin and I read them there." Now, the pastor's plans may be changed for he may be sick and someone else may fill the pulpit, but God's plans do not change. He says that certain things are going to happen and we know they will come to pass. So in the matter of prophecy let us go to God's great bulletin, the Bible, and as we study it we can say, "I know that these things are going to happen because God has made an announcement of them here in His Book."

In my first chapter I told you what would happen when Jesus comes in the air. I wrote of the sounds that would accompany His coming, of how He would appear in the air, of how the dead would be raised from their graves and the living would be caught up from the earth, and of how Christians would be changed as they went up to meet Jesus in the air. Now, Jesus and all of His loved ones have met in this great company in the air. The next question for our attention is therefore: *What will happen in heaven after Jesus comes in the air?*

I. THEY WILL MOVE INTO HEAVEN TOGETHER

Two great events are now going to take place. They are the Judgment Seat of Christ and the Marriage Supper of the Lamb. I hardly think that these events will occur in the air. I believe that Christ and His saints will move into God's heaven and that these things will occur there.

1. *What a happy throng this will be as they move into heaven!* Jesus will be happy because by His shed blood He

has saved multitudes of sinners. He said, "And I, if I be lifted up from the earth, will draw all men unto me." He was lifted up on the Cross and He has been drawing men since that time. Not all of them have responded to His magnetic power, but all of them have been drawn. Some of you who read this book have felt the drawing power of Christ and have resisted Him. You are still lost in your sins, but, thank God, in every country under the sun multitudes of people have surrendered to Him, and at that time they will all be up there with Him after He comes in the air.

Who will be with Him? All those who believed on Him on earth will be with Him. Some will have gone through the process called death and some who were alive when He came will have been caught up to meet Him in the air. At that hour not one of His saints will be missing. Preachers beg God's children to attend the services of the church, but, although there may be large crowds, there are always some members missing. But, my friends, when He comes with a shout and calls His own unto Him, not one of His children will be missing.

The great multitude will be happy, too. They have been saved, but some of them have been beset by Satan; they have been mystified by the troubles of life and some of them have even doubted their salvation. But in that day there will be no more doubt. They will know that heaven is their home, that they are saved and that the devil can never get to them again. Some of that throng have suffered on earth; their bodies have been racked with pain and disease. Then they shall have glorified bodies and they will never suffer again. Surely it will be a happy throng! Down here we think of Jesus and we want to know just what He is like. By faith we have known Him in a small measure, but in that day we shall see Him face to face and we shall know Him as He is. Oh, what glory will be ours when we see Jesus our Saviour!

When I was a little boy my heart was thrilled by the pictures of the Capitol of the United States as they appeared in my geography textbook. I was patriotic and I wanted to see the Capitol. I wanted to look upon that glistening dome, which is such a fitting symbol of our American life. However, I did not go to Washington until I was thirty-two. As I rode into the city I could see the dome of the Capitol clearly outlined against the sky. My heart was thrilled for I was now seeing that which I had longed to see for so many years. Oh, but there is something greater than that! Here in the Bible I read of Jesus and in my heart I have a picture of Him, but when I see Him face to face the experience will be a million times more wonderful than anything of which I have dreamed. We are often disappointed with earthly things, but we will never be disappointed with Him. In this world anticipation is often greater than realization . . . when we see Jesus He will exceed our fondest expectations.

2. *The great throng will be clean . . . inside and out.* Their robes will be washed white in the blood of the Lamb. The dead will be raised incorruptible, the living will be changed, and there will be no wrong thing in any human being because each will then be like Jesus.

When He was upon the earth He made a triumphant entry into Jerusalem. The crowds shouted their hosannas and strewed their garments before Him. But His joy was not complete at that time for the Cross still loomed darkly over His life. But His joy will be absolutely complete when that great procession moves into heaven, for the crown will be before Him and not the Cross. Here on earth suffering awaited Him, but there in heaven sovereignty awaits Him. He will remember the Cross and rejoice that He went all the way to Calvary. "He shall see of the travail of his soul, and shall be satisfied."

As we look at this great throng, Jesus and all of His loved ones, moving into heaven, we cry out, "Oh, what a sight ... Oh, what a day!" Will you be in that great throng or will you be down on the earth facing the Great Tribulation, the Great White Throne and hell?

II. THEN COMES THE JUDGMENT SEAT OF CHRIST

Please remember that only saints will appear before the Judgment Seat. Not one single lost sinner will be there ... they will appear later at the Great White Throne. Some people have the idea that you must wait until you stand at the Judgment Seat before your salvation is determined. No, my friends, we are saved or lost right here on earth. The Judgment Seat is not a judgment of salvation or damnation, but a judgment of rewards.

Paul said, "There is therefore now no condemnation to them which are in Christ Jesus." He has been with Christ for more than eighteen hundred years. He will not be forced to come to this judgment and to have a decision made as to whether or not he is saved or lost. His salvation came to him right here on the earth. If men are already saved upon the earth, what then is the purpose of the Judgment Seat?

1. *At the Judgment Seat we come into complete harmony with Christ.* Even though you are a Christian, saved and born again, it may be that there is something between you and Christ. There may be a secret sin in your life, even though you belong to Him. At the Judgment Seat even the memory of that sin will be put away and there will be nothing between your soul and the Saviour. Heaven is a place of fellowship and where there are differences there can be no fellowship. So at the Judgment Seat every difference will be put aside and there will be perfect harmony between the Lord and His people.

2. *At the Judgment Seat all differences between believers will be adjusted.* God's people often have little differences which keep them from being like Christ. It is hard to adjust

these differences on the earth, but it will be easy in that day because we will all be like Him. If we were more like Him here on earth, it would be easier for us to get along with people, but let me add this: I believe it will be better to settle these differences down here so that we will not have them hanging over us when we stand before Christ at the Judgment Seat.

Some years ago I was holding a meeting in a certain Southern town. In the church there were two men who faithfully attended every service, but who would not speak to each other. One man sat on one side of the church and the other man on the other side. One day when my sermon was finished, I saw these two men leave their respective seats and start toward the center of the church. They met in front of the pulpit, threw their arms around each other, and wept and rejoiced together as they settled their differences. You may understand why a great revival soon broke out in that church and community and why many people found their way to the Saviour. If we get right with others here we will not have the shame of coming into His presence with any trouble between us and others.

In Isaiah 52:8 we read these words, "They shall see eye to eye." That is the way it will be as we stand before the Judgment Seat . . . there will be nothing between us and Christ and no differences between us and others. We will look at everything with the eyes of our Saviour.

3. *At the Judgment Seat we will receive our rewards.* "And, behold, I come quickly; and my reward is with me, to give every man according as his work shall be" (Revelation 22:12).

The Greek word which is translated "judgment seat" is *bema*. In the Grecian world the *bema* was not the bench upon which the judge sat to pass sentence upon the criminal, but it was the throne upon which the judge sat when he distributed prizes to the winners of various games. Now, here is the Christian upon the earth; he is saved by grace and in that day he is going to be rewarded according to his works. In that day all of his works will have ended, the returns will be in and Jesus will judge those works. If they have been good works, the Christian will receive a reward. If those works have not glorified God there will be no reward, but the Christian will squeeze into heaven "yet so as by fire."

In I Corinthians 3:11-15 we are told about the kinds of works which will endure. Every man's works will be tried by the fires of judgment. Some will receive a reward, but some will incur the loss of all their works, though they themselves will be barely saved.

Paul likens the Christian life to a building. If we put rotten material in that building it will perish in the day of judgment. If you serve God only to have a high place among men, your works will perish. If you give your money simply to be seen of men, your works will perish. If you get angry and quit your church when everything does not suit you, your works will be destroyed. If your works consist of criticisms and complaints, they will perish. Everything that is not done in a sweet, unselfish, Christian spirit for the glory of God will perish in that great day. But if you have used your talents well, and have redeemed the time rightly, Christ will have a great reward waiting for you.

There are two kinds of materials. First we think of the gold, silver and precious stones. These materials represent divine things . . . things no man can grow of himself for they come from God alone. So it is that our works which shall stand are those which grow out of the divine nature within us. The other material is spoken of as wood, hay and stubble. These things come about through natural growth. So it is that the works performed by the flesh and for our own glory will be burned to ashes in that day.

Here is a wealthy man who gives ten thousand dollars to get his name before many people. His gift will be burned in that day, but a dime given for the Lord's sake by some poor saint will shine like the stars in heaven. Here is another man who has a great position in the church. He does his work for the love of self and his own glory. His work will be burned up in that day, but the obscure yet true service of some humble saint will last forever and ever.

In I Corinthians 4:4 we read: "He that judgeth me is the Lord." Men try to judge here, but they do not understand. He will be the judge there . . . He is righteous altogether and His judgments will be true.

There are four crowns to be given as rewards. First, there is an incorruptible crown for faithful service. Second, there is a crown of righteousness for those who love His appearing. Third, there is a crown of glory for the faithful preachers. And fourth, there is a crown of life, which is a special martyr's crown.

Paul in his time looked upon the games engaged in by the Grecians. The winner of a contest was always given a crown. A garland of leaves was fitted about his head, but these leaves soon withered. Some day Christ will give His rewards and His crowns to those who have served Him. These crowns will never wither, but will last forever and ever. So it will be a good thing for you to measure your life today, my Christian friend. Are you busy for Jesus? Are you building out of good material? Are you giving yourself to a service that will last when the world is gone?

When I was a little boy my older brother and sister took me to the church one Christmas Eve. A large Christmas tree had been placed in the church and Santa Claus was there distributing presents to all the children. I knew what I wanted from that tree . . . I wanted a drum! I wanted to march up and down the streets and play that drum and enjoy every sound I could get from it. I sat there on the front seat of the church and waited. Santa Claus took down one present after another from the tree. It seemed to me that he called the name of every boy and girl in town, and that he would never call my name. Finally, however, he brought down a present from the topmost bough of the tree, and in a moment he called my name. I rushed forward and received my gift. It was a drum which my sister and brother had placed upon the tree for me. It did not take much in those days to satisfy a little boy's heart, and I was the happiest lad in all the town. Oh, may God help us to give our best in this world to Jesus so that as we stand before Him out yonder we shall hear Him say, "Well done." And as we receive our rewards we shall find the greatest happiness that can come to a human heart.

4. *At the Judgment Seat our ranks in the coming kingdom will be determined.* On October 9, 1942, my wife and I journeyed to Columbus, Mississippi, to see our older son, Walter, receive his wings as a pilot in the Army Air Corps and his commission as a lieutenant. After the wings and commissions had been given out the young men were assigned to their various places of service. Our son was sent to Louisiana to fly the twin-engined bombers in which the navigation students would learn their profession. Now, in the coming millennial kingdom there will be many various places and types of service, and, in like manner after the rewards have been distributed, Christ will assign us to our places and ranks of service.

In that day Jesus will say, "Thou hast been faithful over a few things, I will make thee ruler over many things." If we have suffered with Him, "we shall also reign with him." In the day when Jesus begins to reign in all of His glory, He will give every one of His followers a place of service with Him. A woman said to me some time ago, "I am not interested in a big place in heaven. If I can just slip in the gate and have a very tiny corner I will be satisfied." But, my friends, if we serve Him faithfully here in this world, He will give us more than that . . . He will give us a place of honor and service in the coming kingdom.

III. Then Will Come the Marriage Supper of the Lamb

In Revelation 19:7-9 we read:

> Let us be glad and rejoice, and give honour to him: for the marriage of the Lamb is come, and his wife hath made herself ready. And to her was granted that she should be arrayed in fine linen, clean and white: for the fine linen is the righteousness of the saints. And he saith unto me, Write, Blessed are they which are called unto the marriage supper of the Lamb. And he saith unto me, These are the true sayings of God.

Jesus is the Bridegroom . . . the Church, the company of believers, is the bride. Now, a marriage supper is a time of joy and festivity, and so I believe that this simply means a period of mutual joy, harmony and love. Everything will be right between the Lord and the believers, and everything will be right between the believers themselves. Then will come the climax . . . the completion of happiness for Christ and all those who are saved. Let me give you some facts about the Marriage Supper.

1. *The Groom, Jesus, has the bride, the Church, presented to Him.* We read in Ephesians 5:25-27:

> . . . even as Christ also loved the church, and gave himself for it; that he might sanctify and cleanse it with the washing of water by the word, that he might present it to himself a glorious church, not having spot, or wrinkle, or any such thing; but that it should be holy and without blemish.

The word "present" used here means to "set alongside of." So Jesus will "set us alongside of" Himself and we shall share His glory forever. He said that it would be a "glorious" Church. This means that it will be an exalted Church, exalted to the highest position. He said there would be no spots. This means that all of the sins of believers will be gone. He said there would be no wrinkles. This means that there will be no old age in heaven . . . that we shall be young forever. In other words, "we shall be like him."

2. *A wedding feast means union.* The bride and groom have already been joined together. I have been to wedding feasts and have seen the bride and groom sitting together at a table, holding hands. Each looked into the other's face and had no eyes for anyone else. They had no desire to eat. They were simply supremely happy in the great fact of being joined together . . . "They twain shall be one flesh." So then there shall be great happiness in that hour in heaven when we sit down at the wedding feast. All separations will be past and Jesus and His bride will have been joined together forever.

Here is a man who sails the seven seas. Finally he falls in love with a beautiful young woman and one day as he starts toward his ship he says, "This is positively the last trip. Soon I will come home and we shall marry and then I will go sailing no more." She waits for many months and every month seems to be a year to her. Out yonder on the high seas he feels the same way. But one day his ship comes home and the young woman meets him at the dock. The plans are soon made and they are married. They sit down at the supper together and rejoice that all his traveling days are done and that they are together, united at last forever. Well, my friends, Jesus, our Lover, has gone away for a time, but He said He was coming back. We are to watch, to work, to witness and to wait. Some day He is coming again in the air. He will sit with us at the marriage table and we will rejoice together because all separations will then be over forever.

3. *We shall have perfect harmony at the supper.* All of us will be like Jesus, so there will be no discords. Suppose that a bride and groom came to a banquet right after their marriage and refused to speak to each other. That would

be ridiculous, would it not? Harmony always rules at the marriage supper, because that harmony has been arranged already in a mutual love. So it is that all will be harmony when at last we are at home with Jesus.

We have many denominations in the world now. I think this is necessary because we do not see all things alike, but in that day we shall see everything in its true light, and there will be no differences. We will not be Baptists, Methodists, Presbyterians and others . . . we shall be the children at home with Him.

In Revelation 19:8 we are told that the bride will "be arrayed in fine linen, clean and white." This is the symbol of purity. Can you imagine a bride coming to the marriage supper wearing a dirty dress? Of course not. So when we go to sit down at the Great Supper with Him our garments will be clean and white . . . they will be "washed . . . white in the blood of the Lamb."

At the Marriage Supper some may sit closer to Him than others, for at a marriage supper on this earth the best man and the bridesmaids usually sit closer to the happy couple than the other attendants. This is pleasing to everybody, because that is their rightful place. Now, at the great Marriage Supper of the Lamb, it is probable that Peter, John and Paul will sit closer to Christ than some of us. This, too, will be pleasing to everybody for we shall look at everything in the right way and we know that that is their rightful place. The whole scene will be one of blessing and joy, and all sorrow and pain and death will be gone forever. We shall be joined to Jesus and we shall know that we are going to live with Him throughout all eternity and that the devil can never touch us again. Oh, my friends, will that not be a wonderful day?

4. *The wedding knot will never be broken.* They are often broken in this world, sometimes by divorce and sometimes by death. But our union with Christ can never be

broken. Death will never come to separate Him from us, and disappointment will never come between Him and us.

So this is what will happen in heaven after Jesus comes in the air. We shall move into heaven with Christ and we shall face His Judgment Seat, where we shall be brought into complete harmony with Him. Here our differences will all be adjusted and we shall receive our rewards and be assigned our ranks in the coming kingdom. Then after everything is lovely and in perfect harmony, we shall go into an everlasting period of joy and happiness in the company of Jesus and all the redeemed saints of glory.

Now, all these future joys will begin for us when Jesus comes in the air. If you are not His all the terrors of hell and the wrath of God await you. How is it going to be with you? Are you going to be ready when the great day comes?

Some years ago I preached the funeral sermon for a little baby in North Carolina. The mother was sick at the time and could not leave her bed. The little white casket was brought into her room in order that she might look for the last time into the face of her little baby. As the casket was wheeled out of the room, she cried out, "Good-bye, darling, I will never see you again!" We need never say a thing like this if we know Christ as our Saviour, for then we can be assured of the fact that we will see our loved ones again. When you leave your loved ones will it be forever? Will you go down into the bottomless pit to be forever separated from all that is good and highest and best . . . in other words, to be separated from Christ forever? Or will you mount up to be with Him and to share all the good things that He has for you? Jesus is coming . . . are you ready?

3

WHAT WILL HAPPEN ON EARTH WHEN THE CHURCH IS GONE?

> For then shall be great tribulation, such as was not since the beginning of the world to this time, no, nor ever shall be. And except those days should be shortened, there should no flesh be saved: but for the elect's sake those days shall be shortened (Matthew 24:21-22).

IN THE first chapter of this book I told you what will happen when Jesus comes in the air. We noted the sounds: the victorious shout of Jesus, the voice of the archangel and the trump of God. We thought together of how the dead in Christ will rise first, incorruptible, and then how the living saints, transformed into His likeness, will be taken together with them and be united with Jesus in the air. In the second chapter I told you what will happen in heaven after Jesus comes in the air. We thought together of how Christ and the believers will move into heaven, where every believer will first appear before the Judgment Seat of Christ, and will then sit down with Him at the Marriage Supper of the Lamb. Now we see Jesus and the saints safe in heaven. May God grant that we shall be with them.

But what will then happen upon the earth? I do not claim to understand it all—there have been many different interpretations concerning the events of this period—but from our study I hope that I can bring to you a simple definite outline of these events. Most of all, I want to warn the lost and urge them to come to Christ so that they will not be here upon the earth during this awful period.

I. This Will Not Be the End of the World

Some people think that everything will be over then, that the world will be burned and all the people will be gone. No, the world will still be here and millions of lost people will be here upon the earth. The true Church, which means all those who have been saved through faith in Christ, will have gone up in glory to be with Jesus. This will be the end of the age. The period of grace will be over, but this will not be the end of the world.

II. Dead Unbelievers Will Be Left in Their Graves

In Revelation 20:5 we read:

> But the rest of the dead lived not again until the thousand years were finished.

It is not time for them to rise yet. They will rise a thousand years later and go up to face the Great White Throne and be cast into the lake of fire.

III. Living Unbelievers Will Be Left on the Earth

These people had their chance; Christ called them, but they refused His salvation. Now the Holy Spirit will be gone and there will be no more calls and no more opportunities. They will be left here to face the Great Tribulation while the saved will have gone to be with Jesus.

IV. Now Comes the Tribulation Period

This is the interval of time between the two comings of Christ. He comes first in the air to take up all of His saints, and after the period is over He comes back with them in glory. Bible scholars everywhere say that this period of time is approximately seven years. The last part of the period, that is, the final three and a half years, is called "The

Great Tribulation." Let us look at some of the marks of this period.

1. *The consternation of the world.* The saints will be gone . . . their going will be secret and quick. At His appearing, in the twinkling of an eye, they will mysteriously disappear. There will be no time for farewell notes to be left behind for loved ones to read. There will be vacant chairs in many homes and vacant desks in many offices. Clerks will be gone from the stores. Factory managers will find gaps in their assembly lines. Some of the thrones of the world will be vacant. Now, this is not a local thing . . . it will be world-wide. It will affect every country under the sun. Imagine the amazement of those who are left behind . . . think of the panic that will paralyze many places. Here will be a man searching for his wife . . . for years she had prayed for him and tried to win him to Christ, but he continued to live in his sin and unbelief. Now the husband is searching for her and she is gone.

We read in Luke 17:34-36 these words:

> I tell you, in that night there shall be two men in one bed; the one shall be taken, and the other shall be left. Two women shall be grinding together; the one shall be taken, and the other left. Two men shall be in the field; the one shall be taken, and the other left.

It will be night in some places and people will be sleeping. It will be day in other places and people will be working in the mills and in the fields. This covers both sides of the world. We talk about the manpower shortage of today, but then every industry will be crippled. The churches will still be here but the real Christians will be gone and the pseudo-Christians will try to carry on the work. Business will come to a stand-still for a while and governments and schools will have to be reorganized. At last the world will realize the value of a true Christian. He is the "salt of the earth," but now the salt will be gone. The earth will be in a terrible mess.

Those who are left in the world will wonder and question. Someone will say: "I know what has happened. I attended a church one night and heard the preacher telling about what would happen when Jesus comes . . . this must be it." Although this great truth is preached everywhere now, men are indifferent to it. Then, however, the whole world will know what has come to pass. Today the world scoffs and sneers when we tell them of the Second Coming, but in that day they will know that it is true.

Where are you going to be? Today you have no time for God . . . you are too busy with the things of the world. ". . . what shall it profit a man, if he gain the whole world" and in that day be left behind while God's people go up to meet the Saviour? Oh, flee to Jesus now! This is the day of your salvation and of your opportunity. Tomorrow may be too late. Come to Jesus today.

2. *The hopeless condition of those who are left behind.* Some people will be stirred by these events. They will seek the salvation of their souls. They will remember the sermons they have heard and they will cry out for mercy, but it will be too late then, and they will seek in vain. The door of mercy will be closed and the Lord will laugh at them. You laugh and scoff at Christianity now, but in that day God will do the laughing. Read Proverbs 1:24-29:

> Because I have called, and ye refused; I have stretched out my hand, and no man regarded; but ye have set at nought all my counsel, and would none of my reproof: I also will laugh at your calamity; I will mock when your fear cometh; when your fear cometh as desolation, and your destruction cometh as a whirlwind; when distress and anguish cometh upon you. Then shall they call upon me, but I will not answer; they shall seek me early, but they shall not find me: for that they hated knowledge, and did not choose the fear of the Lord.

You may sow now, but you will reap then. You may leave God out now . . . some sin stands between you and the Saviour . . . but in that day you will call upon Him, and He will not hear. Oh, my friends, He will hear you now. Call upon Him without delay and be saved from the awful penalty of your sin!

In the seventh chapter of Revelation we are told that a great multitude will be saved out of the Great Tribulation. This multitude will probably consist of many Jews who will be wondrously saved and also of many people from the far parts of the earth who had never before heard of Jesus. However, it is almost certain that none of those who rejected Christ during the Gospel Age will be among the number saved.

Read II Thessalonians 2:11-12:

> And for this cause God shall send them strong delusion, that they should believe a lie: that they all might be damned who believed not the truth, but had pleasure in unrighteousness.

Men who will not believe now in the truth which is in Christ Jesus, will then believe the lies of Antichrist and there will be no chance for salvation after Jesus comes.

In Ezekiel 8:18 we learn how God deals with disobedient people:

> Therefore will I also deal in fury: mine eye shall not spare, neither will I have pity: and though they cry in mine ears with a loud voice, yet will I not hear them.

My unsaved friend, you are in peril. If you will not come to the Saviour now, your doom will be sealed when He comes again. There is no middle ground. "He that believeth on the Son hath everlasting life: and he that believeth not the Son shall not see life; but the wrath of God abideth on him" (John 3:36).

3. *God's dealings with the world in this period.* Now we shall see why this period is called a "time of trouble" and the "Great Tribulation."

(a) *He will avenge the death of His blessed Son.* We read that God has a "controversy with the nations." Why does He have such a controversy? Surely it is because all nations shared in the awful crime of His crucifixion. Jesus was reviled here, but He opened not His mouth. In that day God will say, "Vengeance is mine; I will repay." He will have ample reason for paying, and, believe me, God knows how to pay. We live in a world that is stained by the blood of God's dear Son. All the world lies guilty before Him. In every generation men add to this guilt by crucifying afresh the Son of God. God is withholding His judgment now, but in that day He shall avenge the death of Christ. Read Zephaniah 1:14-18:

> The great day of the Lord is near, it is near, and hasteth greatly, even the voice of the day of the Lord: the mighty man shall cry there bitterly. That day is a day of wrath, a day of trouble and distress, a day of wasteness and desolation, a day of darkness ... And I will bring distress upon men, that they shall walk like blind men, because they have sinned against the Lord: and their blood shall be poured out as dust, and their flesh as the dung. Neither their silver nor gold shall be able to deliver them in the day of the Lord's wrath.

(b) *Peace shall be taken from the earth.* We have no peace now, but the wars of today are just a shadow of the things to come. In fact, the troubles of the tribulation period will be the troubles which we have now, multiplied a billion times. Today there are few countries which are not in war, but in that day all nations will be killing each other. "And there went out another horse that was red: and power was given him that sat thereon to take peace from the earth, and that they should kill one another: and there was given unto him a great sword" (Revelation 6:4).

Today Christians are the salt of the earth . . . they are preserving the race from corruption. Today the Holy Spirit is restraining the evil influences of the world, but in that day He shall be gone and all the passions of hell will be loosed. It will be the time of slaughter and bloodshed. Suppose that right now all Christian influence, churches, individual Christians, and all law and order were removed from our cities . . . they would be cities like unto hell. Well, in that day all the earth will be like hell.

(c) *The necessities of life will be sold at famine prices.* We see a few of these conditions in Revelation 6:5-6:

> And when he had opened the third seal, I heard the third beast say, Come and see. And I beheld, and lo a black horse; and he that sat on him had a pair of balances in his hand. And I heard a voice in the midst of the four beasts say, A measure of wheat for a penny, and three measures of barley for a penny; and see thou hurt not the oil and the wine.

Henry McLemore, an American correspondent in London, recently told of paying $1.75 for one peach. He said that in his boyhood days he worked in the peach packing plants of Georgia, where he had seen bushels of luscious peaches going to waste. Throughout the centuries God has given abundant crops to man and has received little thanks in return. In the days of the Great Tribulation there will be an awful scarcity of food and multitudes will die of starvation.

(d) *The pale horse of death will ride roughshod through the world.* In Revelation 6:8 we are told that death will come riding with hades following him. Death seizes the body and hades seizes the soul. At that time one fourth of the inhabitants of the earth will die.

(e) *There will be fearful convulsions of nature.* You will find this picture in Revelation 6:12-14. Earthquakes will rock the world. The Tokyo earthquake of 1923 will be a tremor in comparison. In that day the mountains will be shaken out of their places; the sun, which has blessed the world through the ages, will be darkened; the moon will become as blood. Throughout the years men have despised the blood of Jesus Christ, but in that day they shall be compelled to look upon blood. In that day they will remember that it is too late for the precious blood of Christ to save them. Even the heavens will show their wrath against the earth by casting their stars upon it. If these things should happen now we would be frightened beyond measure . . . Think then of the fear that will seize the world in that day.

(f) *The world's greatest prayer meeting will be held.* We read in Revelation 6:15-17:

> And the kings of the earth, and the great men, and the rich men, and the chief captains, and the mighty men, and every bondman, and every free man, hid themselves in the dens and in the rocks of the mountains; and said to the mountains and rocks, Fall on us, and hide us from the face of him that sitteth on the throne, and from the wrath of the Lamb: for the great day of his wrath is come; and who shall be able to stand?

Preachers plead with people to come to prayer meetings, where they can offer up their prayers with the hope of an answer. In that day they will cry out, but their prayers will be too late. Many people think that the prayer meeting is beneath their notice and dignity. They feel that they will be considered too religious if they go to prayer meeting on Wednesday night . . . in that day the kings and rulers and great men of the earth will be praying. Today they think prayer is a useless thing . . . then they will cry out for mercy. The preacher warns today of the wrath that is to come and men laugh at him. In that day they will say, "The preacher was right and I was wrong." Alas, then it will be too late!

Notice the object of their prayers. They pray for the rocks to fall upon them and to hide them from the face of

Simple Sermons on the Second Coming

Christ. Now they will not come to the Rock of Ages to find a hiding place from sin, but in that day they will pray for a rock to fall upon them. God's people long now to see the face of Jesus. In that day lost men will pray that they might be hidden from His face.

(g) *God's indignations upon the earth.* I will mention only one or two of these indignations. The first is found in Revelation 9:1-5. In these verses we are told that the bottomless pit will open and that locusts like horses will fly out over all the earth. There will be millions of them and they will have in their bodies the sting of the scorpion. For five months they will torment all those who are living. The sixth verse tells us that "in those days shall men seek death, and shall not find it; and shall desire to die, and death shall flee from them."

In Revelation 16:9-11 we read that the heat will be so great and the suffering so terrible that men will gnaw their tongues in pain. On the Cross the blessed Jesus cried out, "I thirst." There was no relief for Him, except in death. In that day men will thirst and there will be no relief for them and no death. What a terrible period this is going to be! Again I warn you to flee from the wrath which is to come.

4. *In the same period the Antichrist will be manifested.* This great, prominent, wicked being will move upon the earth. He is called Antichrist, which means that he is opposed to all that Christ stands for.

(a) *Let us look at his nature.* He is a real man as Jesus was a real man. Jesus was a dual personality . . . He was born of God and man. The Antichrist will be a dual personality . . . he will be both Satan and man. Some scholars interpret Daniel 11:37 as teaching that he will be a Jew. He will be a superman, the son of the devil with all of the devil's power. As Jesus was the Seed of a woman, so will Antichrist be the seed of the devil. Some people point to Hitler and other present-day world characters as being antichrists, but the Bible plainly teaches that the Antichrist will not be revealed until after the Rapture. One of these characters may readily merge into the Antichrist, but we cannot say now that any living man is the Antichrist. Revelation 11:7 seems to teach that he is now in the bottomless pit and will come out upon the earth during the tribulation period.

(b) *He may be Judas reincarnated.* In his life Judas was against everything that Christ stood for . . . so will the Antichrist be against all that Jesus stood for.

Judas was more than a man . . . he was a devil, according to the words of Jesus in John 6:70: "Have not I chosen you twelve, and one of you is a devil?" Jesus was God incarnate and Judas was the devil incarnate. Jesus called Judas the son of perdition and in Revelation we are told that the Antichrist is the son of perdition.

In Acts 1:25 we read that Judas went to his "own place." This is not said of any other character in the Bible. The Antichrist will come up out of the bottomless pit. Could this be the place to which Jesus referred? In Revelation 17:8 we are told that the Antichrist was and is not, but that he will come up out of the bottomless pit and go into perdition. Judas was and is not, he has gone to his own place and is called the son of perdition. The devil used him once . . . could it be that he will use him again? It may be that Judas will be the Antichrist.

(c) *Contrasts between Christ and the Antichrist.* There is a contrast in names . . . one is the Christ and the other is the Antichrist. One is the Man of Sorrows . . . the other is the man of sin. One is the Son of God . . . the other is the son of perdition. One is the Seed of the woman . . . the other is the seed of the serpent. One is the Lamb . . . the other is a beast. One is the Holy One . . . the other is the unholy one. One is the Truth . . . the other one is a lie. One is the Prince of Peace . . . the other is a profane prince. One is the Glorious Branch . . . the other is the abominable branch. One is the Good Shepherd . . . the other is the idol shepherd. One is the Mighty Angel . . . the other is the angel from the bottomless pit.

There is a contrast in character and career. Christ came down from heaven . . . the Antichrist will come up from the bottomless pit. Christ came in Another's name . . . the Antichrist will come in his own name. Christ came to do the will of God . . . the Antichrist will come to do his own will. Christ wrought in the power of the Holy Spirit . . . the Antichrist will be energized by Satan. Christ submitted Himself to God . . . the Antichrist will defy God. Christ humbled Himself . . . the Antichrist will exalt himself. Christ honored God, His Father . . . the Antichrist will refuse to honor Him. Christ cleansed the Temple . . . the Antichrist will defile the Temple. Christ ministered to the needy . . . the Antichrist will make the people needy. Christ was rejected of men . . . the Antichrist will be accepted by all the world. Christ led the flock . . . the Antichrist will leave the flock. Christ was slain for the people . . . the Antichrist will slay the people. Christ glorified God . . . the Antichrist will blaspheme God. Christ was received up into heaven . . . the Antichrist will be cast into the lake of fire.

(d) *The career of the Antichrist.* He will pose as a great religious leader and bring about an amalgamation of all the churches. We see the shadow of this event in the various union movements which are proposed today. There are certain religious groups who do not even believe in the divinity of Christ. Other groups are saying: "These things do not matter. Let us go together and present a solid front to the world." So will it be in that day when the Antichrist will bring all the churches together in a great federation. The pope with his great world system is another shadow of things which will come to pass in the religious realm under the Antichrist.

The Antichrist will become the political head of the revived Roman Empire. Rome was once the proud mistress of the world, and under the Antichrist those nations which formed the Roman Empire will again be strong and mighty. He will create an international league of nations and be a world king. His reign will be a brutal dictatorship. Many people will suffer under his lash. Hitler is a puppet compared with the Antichrist.

He will exercise intellectual superiority and will be a being of great wisdom. He will perform many mighty miracles. He will be sharp as a serpent and with his power he will cause men everywhere to follow him. You see the devil is a mighty being and he will energize the Antichrist and enable him to do almost anything on earth.

He will be a mighty warrior and statesman. He will conquer countries and topple kings from their thrones. He will take over all these countries as supreme dictator. This sounds very much like the things Hitler has done, so I tell you again that there are many shadows in the world today which point to things yet to come.

He will deceive the Jews at first and pose as their Messiah. They will swallow him and all of his schemes. They did not accept Jesus when He came into the world as a suffering servant, but when this one comes into it as a mighty king they will make a treaty with him.

The first three and one-half years of his reign will be bad enough, but the last period will indeed be "the Great Tribulation." The devil is in the air now as the "prince of the power of the air," but by that time he will be cast down upon the earth, and as the Holy Spirit possessed and filled Jesus, so will Satan possess and fill the Antichrist. The Holy Trinity is composed of God the Father, God the Son and God the Holy Spirit. The unholy trinity of that period will be composed of Satan; the Antichrist, his man on earth; and the false prophet, who will have the same relationship to the Antichrist as the Holy Spirit does to Christ.

He will rebuild the Temple at Jerusalem and set himself up as God. In II Thessalonians 2:4 we read:

> Who opposeth and exalteth himself above all that is called God, or that is worshipped; so that he as God sitteth in the temple of God, shewing himself that he is God.

Then he will set up his image in the Temple and command the Jews to worship it. Those who do not worship this image will be put to death. In the beginning of this period he will appear to the Jews as an angel of light . . . now they will see him in his true colors. He denies God and God's Son . . . he does all that he can to exterminate God's people, the Jews . . . he destroys their method of worship and everything that bears witness to the existence of an Almighty God.

There are many Scriptures which describe the Antichrist and his work. The language of today is not sufficient to tell us of all his wickedness. Great multitudes will be slain, but God will marvelously preserve one hundred and forty-four thousand Jews. Psalm 91:3 reads: "He shall deliver thee from the snare of the fowler."

(e) *A brief look at the Jews during this period.* We are told that at the beginning of the period, the Jews will look upon the Antichrist as their friend. He will make a seven-year treaty with them. He will help them to return to Jerusalem to build the Temple and to set up their worship there. However, the last part of the period will be one of intense suffering for the Jews. They will endure all manner of persecution. They have suffered much in Germany, but their sufferings of the present day are not to be compared with the sufferings of that period. Here is another shadow of things to come.

A remnant of the Jews will preach the Gospel of the kingdom. Today we preach the Gospel of grace. We tell men that a Saviour died for them and that He will receive those who come to Him by faith. In that period the Church will have been taken up and the world will be looking toward the time when Jesus will come back in glory. The message then will be, "Repent: for the kingdom of heaven is at hand." The Holy Spirit will come upon these Jews as He did upon Moses and Noah. The Jews are well-fitted for the task of preaching the Gospel of the kingdom for they are now scattered all over the world and they speak the languages of many countries. In that day God will remove their blindness and use them as evangelists.

Two witnesses will then come upon the scene and will preach mightily wherever they go. Who are these two witnesses? We are told that one has the power to shut up the heavens and that reminds us of Elijah. We are told that the other has the power to turn water into blood, and immediately we think of Moses. Moses and Elijah may be these two witnesses. They will go up and down the land for twelve hundred and sixty days testifying for God. We can see that even then in that dark period God will not leave Himself without witnesses. These are the two great evangelists and the one hundred and forty-four thousand Jews will be the lesser evangelists. However, the Antichrist soon will kill these two witnesses. God will then raise them up and translate them into heaven as He did once before.

(f) *The end of the tribulation period.* Things on the earth will have come to their very worst stage. The Antichrist will have the upper hand. In his conceit he will come to think that he can defeat God and set himself up as sovereign over heaven and earth. So he will gather all the kingdoms of the earth together to fight against the Lord God Almighty. There is just One who can stop him and put all his work to naught and punish him forever . . . He is the King of kings and Lord of lords. It will be time then for Him to come back in glory and to put an end to the tribulation period. I shall try to tell you about this in the next chapter.

There is a lesson in the Great Tribulation which I must emphasize. It is an awful period and it is my duty as a servant of Christ to warn you about the wrath which is to come. There is only one way for you to escape . . . you must come to Jesus. In contrast to the tribulation what does He offer to do for you in that day? He will come and take you out of this world; He will give you a new body and He will make you perfect in every way. He will restore your loved ones to you, and take you and them into heaven to live with Him in bliss forever. Which will you take? Will it be tribulation, Satan and hell—or Jesus, glory and heaven?

The other day I sat in a doctor's office. This doctor is a splendid Christian man. I looked up in front of me and there upon the wall I saw a little sign and on it were two words, "Perhaps Today." He wanted to remind his patients that Jesus might be coming at any minute. Jesus may come sooner than you expect. *Are you ready?*

4

WHAT WILL HAPPEN WHEN JESUS RETURNS TO THE EARTH IN GLORY?

> And I saw heaven opened, and behold a white horse; and he that sat upon him was called Faithful and True, and in righteousness he doth judge and make war. His eyes were as a flame of fire, and on his head were many crowns; and he had a name written, that no man knew, but he himself. And he was clothed with a vesture dipped in blood: and his name is called the Word of God. And the armies which were in heaven followed him upon white horses, clothed in fine linen, white and clean. And out of his mouth goeth a sharp sword, that with it he should smite the nations: and he shall rule them with a rod of iron: and he treadeth the winepress of the fierceness and wrath of Almighty God. And he hath on his vesture and on his thigh a name written, KING OF KINGS, AND LORD OF LORDS (Revelation 19:11-16).

IN PREVIOUS chapters we have noted what will happen when Jesus comes in the air, what will happen in heaven after His coming in the air, and what will happen on earth after His coming in the air. We saw the Antichrist ruling upon the earth . . . grown so proud and conceited that he had drawn up his armies to fight against the Lord God Almighty. I told you that only One could conquer and punish the Antichrist, and that One is Jesus Christ, the Lord of lords and the King of kings.

Now as the Antichrist draws up his mighty armies for battle upon the earth, we see Christ and His saints and the angels in heaven poised for a descent toward the earth.

I. CHRIST WILL THEN COME TO THE EARTH IN GLORY WITH HIS SAINTS

Remember that this is the second phase of His coming. Approximately seven years before He had come in the air. He had stopped there and caught up the saints to be with Him. Oh, the joy and power in that preposition "with." We shall be *with* Jesus forever. He came the first time in the air *for* His saints . . . He comes this time to the earth *with* His saints.

The first time, when He comes in the air, will be a secret appearing, and only the believers will know about it; but now when He comes back in glory every eye will see Him and everyone will know just who He is.

Oh, my friends, the presence of the Lord is greatly needed upon the earth today! Only He can stop war, and give us permanent peace. Only He can cast out fear and straighten out the sinful earth. Only He can take sickness away and destroy death forever. One look at the world today will convince you how much it does need the mighty presence of Christ. But if the world needs Him now, it will need Him much more in the end of the tribulation period. At that time the Antichrist will be in full power, blaspheming and denying God. All the world will be worshiping him . . . the people will be branded with his mark upon their heads and in their hands. The godly Jewish remnant in its last extremity will be crying out, "How long, O Lord, how long must Thy people suffer?" Here on earth the forces of the Antichrist will be gathered together to try to prevent the Lord Jesus from coming back to earth and claiming His inheritance.

The hour strikes . . . the dreadful moment has come . . . the prophecy in II Thessalonians 1:7-9 is about to be fulfilled:

> And to you who are troubled rest with us, when the Lord Jesus shall be revealed from heaven with his mighty angels, in flaming fire taking vengeance on them that know

not God, and that obey not the gospel of our Lord Jesus Christ: who shall be punished with everlasting destruction from the presence of the Lord, and from the glory of his power.

The nineteenth chapter of Revelation gives us a vivid picture of this coming in glory. Let us now study the passage in detail.

1. *Jesus comes sitting upon a white horse.* The Greek word here intimates that this steed is a war horse of fine mettle. His color is white, an emblem of Christ's purity and holiness. Now note the contrast in His first coming to earth in humility and this coming in glory and power. You remember that the first time He came He was born in a stable where horses are kept at night. This time He comes astride a horse, riding in majesty. The first time he rode into Jerusalem on a little donkey. This time he will enter on a mighty charger. His coming in glory is a direct contrast all the way through to His coming in humility the first time.

2. *He is called "Faithful and True."* Men are not faithful and they do not tell the truth. But here is One who is always "Faithful and True." He is going to keep every promise and be true to every threat that He has made.

The modernists read some harsh things in the Bible and then throw up their hands and say, "These things can never happen . . . He is a God of love." Yes, He is a God of love, but He tells us that when we reject this love and trample Christ under foot and spurn His grace, this love will turn into a mighty wrath and He will punish unbelievers and sinners. I tell you that Jesus is true to every word. You may laugh now, but in that day you will know that His promises are not idle threats.

3. *He comes to "judge."* When He was upon the earth men judged Him. He stood before Caiaphas and Herod and Pilate . . . they convicted Him, the innocent Son of God,

However, in that day He will be the Judge. In Acts 17:31 we read:

> Because he hath appointed a day, in the which he will judge the world in righteousness by that man whom he hath ordained; whereof he hath given assurance unto all men, in that he hath raised him from the dead.

We are told that He will judge "in righteousness." He was not judged that way Himself . . . wicked men trumped up their charges and lied against Him. They could not find Him guilty on a single count. Even Pilate had to say, "I find no fault in this man." Yet they sent Him to a cruel death. When He comes all He does will be right and He will "judge the world in righteousness."

4. *He comes to "make war" on the earth.* On the earth He ministered to all those who were needy. He held His arms out and said unto them, "Come unto me, all ye that labour and are heavy laden, and I will give you rest." But all that will be changed when He comes in glory. He will ride upon a war horse and will come for the express purpose of making war against the hosts of Satan which dare to oppose Him.

God saved Israel at the Red Sea while the hosts of Pharaoh went down to their watery graves. As the children of Israel praised God on the far side of the sea they sang this refrain, "The Lord is a man of war." The modernists and pacifists of today come along and point to the gentleness and sweetness of Jesus and condemn all war in His Name. They ought to study the Bible and not resort to their own fancies. They would learn that there are some wars of righteousness . . . that there is a time to fight and stand up for the cause of Christ. They would then understand that at the proper time and for a proper cause Jesus will make war and destroy multitudes.

5. *His eyes will be as "a flame of fire."* On earth His eyes shone with tenderness and children everywhere were

attracted to Him. He looked at Peter and that look melted Peter's heart and caused him to go out and weep bitterly. He stood at the grave of Lazarus and His eyes were filled with tears. But when He comes in glory His eyes will flash like fire. You see, He will be filled with a holy indignation. He will pierce through all hypocrisy and see man as he is. His eyes will be like a searchlight penetrating every thought and every heart.

6. *He will be bedecked with "many crowns."* On earth He was crowned with a crown of thorns, which is the symbol of a curse. But when He comes again He will be crowned with glory and honor, symbols of His authority. He came before as a lowly man to suffer . . . He will come then as a victorious conqueror. "Many crowns" would mean absolute authority. He will be King, not only of the Jews as Pilate's inscription showed, but King of the Gentiles as well. He will be King of kings and Lord of lords and all the world will be compelled to bow before Him and submit to His universal authority.

7. *He comes with "a name . . . that no man knew, but he himself."* In the Bible names express nature. For instance, the name of Peter meant "a rock." When Jesus comes He will be so majestic and so full of unspeakable glory that He has a name which no man can fathom. There will be such mysterious depths in Him that no man will be able to understand Him.

8. *He comes "clothed with a vesture dipped in blood."* On the Cross His raiment was stained in His own blood. When He comes back to slay offenders He will shed their blood.

9. *He will be called "The Word of God."* No longer will He be called Jesus, which means Saviour, for His saving work will be over. He will be called "The Word of God" . . . His name points to the dignity and majesty and glory of God.

In John 1:1 we read:

> In the beginning was the Word, and the Word was with God, and the Word was God.

This great Eternal One existed before the world was made. When He came to the earth the first time His humanity was most prominent, but in that day His deity will be the most prominent thing about Him.

10. *He comes to "smite the nations" with a sword out of His mouth.* When He was here before, words of blessing and comfort came out of His mouth. In that day a sword will come out to smite the nations. Throughout the years He has sent out the Word to slay the sin in men . . . in that day the Word will go out to slay men in sin. Isaiah 11:4 reads:

> But with righteousness shall he judge the poor, and reprove with equity for the meek of the earth; and he shall smite the earth with the rod of his mouth, and with the breath of his lips shall he slay the wicked.

When He came out of the Garden of Gethsemane Judas kissed Him and the soldiers rushed forward to arrest Him. He said to them, "Whom seek ye?" and they replied, "Jesus of Nazareth." Quietly He said to them, "I am he," and we read that "they went backward, and fell to the ground." If such power could come out of His mouth then, what will it be when He comes in judgment?

11. *He comes to rule the nations "with a rod of iron."* How different is this from the modernists' conception of Him. These people weaken His character and make Him so tender and effeminate that He can never punish sin. But God is not only a God of love; He is holy and righteous. He cannot ignore sin in people . . . He must and will punish it.

Today He deals in grace . . . He implores men to obey Him and love Him. Then the day of grace will be over and He will compel men to obey. The insignia of Christ today is the Cross, and the Cross always reminds us of His submission to death and of His blood shed for us. In that day His insignia will be a rod of iron for He will stand for resistless power. We speak today of the "iron heel of the dictators." Today Jesus, in tenderness, invites men to come and follow Him . . . in that day His tenderness will be turned to wrath. He will crush the head of the serpent and put down all His enemies.

12. *He comes to tread "the winepress of the fierceness and wrath of Almighty God."* In Isaiah 63:3 we read:

> I have trodden the winepress alone; and of the people there was none with me: for I will tread them in mine anger, and trample them in my fury; and their blood shall be sprinkled upon my garments, and I will stain all my raiment.

All the nations of the earth will be gathered under the leadership of the Antichrist to fight against the Lord and His hosts, but He will trample them under foot. Read Revelation 14:20:

> And the winepress was trodden without the city, and blood came out of the winepress, even unto the horse bridles, by the space of a thousand and six hundred furlongs.

For two hundred miles around Armageddon the carnage will be so great that the blood will be up to the horses' bits. We talk today of total war, but Jesus will be the Victor in the greatest battle ever to be fought. All the punishment which He metes out will be fully merited for He has been rejected, and a murderer accepted in His place. God will have been openly blasphemed, but now the Divine Executioner steps forth to do His work and to inflict vengeance upon the blasphemers.

13. *He comes followed by great armies.* We are told in

Revelation 19:14 that these armies will follow Him upon white horses and that they will be "clothed in fine linen, white and clean." These armies will consist of all believers of all ages . . . the saints of God who have washed their robes and made them white in the blood of the Lamb. They went up with Him in the air and now they come back with Him down to the earth. "If we suffer, [with Him] we shall also reign with him." He will come back to reign upon the earth for a thousand years.

I would rather, a billion times, follow Him in that day than be on the earth waiting for His arrival. Those who follow Him will be the people saved forever and safe forever. Those upon the earth will be facing the wrath of a rejected Lord and King. You can get on the right side today if you will believe on Him and receive Him in your heart. This means that in the day of His coming you will be safe. If you will not receive Him as your Saviour, may God have mercy on you in that day.

We now have the picture of the Antichrist and his hosts upon the earth ready to fight the Lord. The heavens will open and Jesus in all of His glory and power will come riding on a white horse, followed by the mighty armies of those who have loved and trusted Him. Of course, a tremendous crash is inevitable . . . the greatest battle of all time will take place.

II. THE BATTLE OF ARMAGEDDON

1. God gets the birds ready to devour the flesh of the dead. Revelation 19:17-19 reads:

> And I saw an angel standing in the sun; and he cried with a loud voice, saying to all the fowls that fly in the midst of heaven, Come and gather yourselves together unto the supper of the great God; that ye may eat the flesh of kings, and the flesh of captains, and the flesh of mighty men, and the flesh of horses, and of them that sit on them, and the flesh of all men, both free and bond,

both small and great. And I saw the beast, and the kings of the earth, and their armies, gathered together to make war against him that sat on the horse, and against his army.

In this passage the word "flesh" is mentioned five times. On the earth men have lived after the flesh and not after the spirit, and now their flesh is going to be literally devoured.

An angel stands in the sun where everybody can see him. He cries with a loud voice so that everyone can hear him. He is getting ready for the slaughter of the armies. He speaks to all the birds of the air, telling them to get ready for the great supper . . . a supper at which they will eat the flesh of all those who are gathering against God.

Millions are going to be slain in this battle and then the millennial kingdom will be set up on the earth. It will not do for the kingdom to begin with a plague which the festering out carcasses would cause, so it is necessary for the birds to get the flesh out of the way. God prepares for everything, does He not?

2. *Next the Antichrist and his false prophet will be "cast alive into a lake of fire."* They will be the first to go into this place. A thousand years later Satan will be cast into the lake, and then all of his believers will join him there. We note that these two great world powers are "cast alive" into the lake of fire. They are not killed but they are put in there alive to suffer forever and to pay for their rebellion against God.

The Antichrist does not have a chance to lead his army against the Lord. Scripture simply tells us that he was taken and cast into the lake of fire. He boasted of his power! He defied God! He was going to throw Him from His throne! But the great Christ merely moved His hand and all of the Antichrist's vaunted power was gone, and he was cast into the lake of fire.

Men today are defying God. They laugh at the thought of Him and go on headlong in their sins. God warns them of their fate and they say, "I am the master of my fate; I am the captain of my soul." But as God took the Antichrist and the false prophet and brought them down, someday with the greatest of ease He will bring these sinners down from their high places and cast them into the lake of fire.

The leaders are now gone, but their armies are left. They do not last a minute. They do not get a chance to fire one bullet or to make one charge. The sword proceeds out of the mouth of that mighty One on the horse; this sword cuts them all down and they die in their tracks. Millions and millions die . . . no wonder there is blood for two hundred miles around.

Come on, ye birds . . . God has given you your orders. We read in Ezekiel 39:17:

> And, thou son of man, thus saith the Lord God; Speak unto every feathered fowl, and to every beast of the field, Assemble yourselves, and come; gather yourselves on every side to my sacrifice that I do sacrifice for you, even a great sacrifice upon the mountains of Israel, that ye may eat flesh, and drink blood.

You ride down the highway and on the side of the road you see an animal which has been killed by a car. The odor of the decaying flesh is a stench in your nostrils. Maybe one or two vultures are pulling the carcass to pieces and it is a horrible sight in your eyes. How much more awful then will be that sight after the battle of Armageddon! There will be a line of dead bodies two hundred miles long, with the scavengers of the air greedily devouring their flesh. This is a picture of what sin brings. You cannot defy God Almighty and reject His Son Jesus Christ and get away with it.

III. A NATION WILL BE BORN IN A DAY

This will be the Jewish nation . . . God's own people. In Zechariah 12:10 we read:

> And I will pour upon the house of David, and upon the inhabitants of Jerusalem, the spirit of grace and of supplications: and they shall look upon me whom they have pierced, and they shall mourn for him, as one mourneth for his only son, and shall be in bitterness for him, as one that is in bitterness for his firstborn.

Israel rejected Christ and pierced Him. On that day Israel will recognize the Messiah. The veil will be lifted from her eyes. She will repent of her sin and return unto the Lord. Once, in the days of David and Solomon, Israel was a mighty nation. That nation fell because of its sin and because of its rejection of Jesus Christ. Today there are Jews all over the world, but there is no Jewish nation. But in that day there will again be a Jewish nation called Israel, centered in Jerusalem, with Jesus reigning on the throne of David as King of the Jews. This does not necessarily mean individual salvation for every Jew living. I believe it does mean, however, that Israel will be one of the nations which will live through the kingdom age of the millennium with Jesus as her Sovereign.

IV. Then Comes the Judgment of the Nations

Jesus will come down to the earth, stand upon the Mount of Olives and judge the living nations. In Matthew 25:31-33 we read:

> When the Son of man shall come in his glory, and all the holy angels with him, then shall he sit upon the throne of his glory: and before him shall be gathered all nations: and he shall separate them one from another, as a shepherd divideth his sheep from the goats: and he shall set the sheep on his right hand, but the goats on the left.

All the saints will assist Him. Note I Corinthians 6:2: "Do ye not know that the saints shall judge the world?" Who will be judged? Not individuals, but the nations which are existing when He comes in glory. At the Judgment Seat of Christ believers will be judged and there will necessarily be a resurrection. At the Great White Throne lost sinners will be judged, and of course, there will be another resurrection. However, there is no resurrection in connection with the judgment of the nations . . . He will simply judge the nations which are then in existence. What is the basis of this judgment? It will be on the ground of the treatment which the nations have accorded His Jewish brethren, especially during the tribulation period. Some nations will be saved to go through the kingdom period. You will remember that there will be one hundred and forty-four thousand Jewish evangelists during the tribulation. If the nations have treated them well, clothed them, given them to drink and visited them, these nations shall be saved. "Inasmuch as ye have done it unto one of the least of these my brethren, ye have done it unto me." Jesus will say to them, "Come, ye blessed of my Father, inherit the kingdom prepared for you." This is not the kingdom of heaven, but the millennial kingdom under Christ.

There are some nations that are not treating the Jews rightly . . . we have shadows of this in the world today. To these nations Jesus will say, "Depart from me, ye cursed, into everlasting fire." The Antichrist and the false prophet are already in that fire, and now they will have some company.

Some people quote Matthew 25:31-46 to prove salvation by good deeds. They say that if you help the poor and give to the needy you will be saved. This is definitely not true . . . the judgment here refers only to the nations . . . here they are judged according to the treatment they have given the Jews.

Let us see where we are now. Jesus has come back to the earth in glory. The saints and angels are with Him . . . there He stands on the Mount of Olives. The Antichrist and the false prophet who caused all the trouble during the tribulation period have been cast into the lake of fire. All the armies that were gathered against the Lord have been slain and the birds have eaten their flesh in the great feast. The Jews have looked to Jesus and owned Him as King. Their nation lives again with Jesus as the center of their activities. All the living nations have been judged. Some have been cast into the lake of fire and others have been left to go through the kingdom age of a thousand years.

Are we ready now for the millennium? Are we ready for Christ to reign supreme? Not quite . . . one more thing must take place. Satan and his influence must be throttled . . . so Jesus has him bound and put in a pit which is shut up and sealed over him. Here he must stay for a thousand years. This is only right for there can be no perfection on earth as long as Satan is left here. We are ready now for the one thousand years of peace, prosperity and plenty. I will tell you about that in another chapter. But, before I close this one, may I ask you a question? Are you going to see His glory in that day? You cannot see it if you have not given your heart to Him here. There will be no second opportunity for you. He has done all that is necessary; now everything else is up to you. The choice is clear . . . He holds before you life and death. You can accept Him and be taken up with Him forever. You can reject Him and be left upon the earth to suffer through the Great Tribulation and be cast into the lake of fire. Which shall it be? He gives you the choice today.

An R.A.F. bomber had flown over Germany and on the return trip to England was damaged by enemy fire. The plane reached the home base safely, but several of the crew were injured and were placed in a near-by hospital. One of these men turned to the man in the bed next to his and said, "Say, buddy, can you help me out with a bit of religion?"

The other boy replied, "Sorry, pal, but I never have been the religious kind."

He then turned to the man on the other side and again he

said, "Say, buddy, can you help me out with a bit of religion?"

The man answered: "I don't know much about it, but there is a Salvation Army lassie who comes in here every Thursday. Maybe she can help you out."

"But," replied the wounded lad, "I have a feeling that I will not be here Thursday. I need some help now." He lay still for a few minutes and then said to the man in the next bed, "Buddy, something is going through my mind now. I don't know where I got it, but maybe you can help me. It is something like this, 'Suffer little children . . .' Do you know anything about that?"

"Yes," said the other soldier, "I know that; I learned it in Sunday school. Jesus said it to little children . . . He said, 'Suffer little children to come unto me, and forbid them not: for of such is the kingdom of God.'"

"Say, buddy," asked the wounded lad, "do you think this Lord Jesus, who was interested in little children, would receive me?"

And the other boy said, "I am sure He will. If He loved little children and received them, He would receive you, too, if you just asked Him."

The man pulled the sheet up over his face and prayed his simple prayer. Of course, Jesus received him, for did He not say, "Him that cometh to me I will in no wise cast out"? Before long the soul of this boy went out to be with Jesus, but the smile of heaven was upon his face. Oh, friend, He will receive you, too. Will you not come to Him now?

5

WHAT WILL HAPPEN DURING THE MILLENNIUM?

And I saw an angel come down from heaven, having the key of the bottomless pit and a great chain in his hand. And he laid hold on the dragon, that old serpent, which is the Devil, and Satan, and bound him a thousand years, and cast him into the bottomless pit, and shut him up, and set a seal upon him, that he should deceive the nations no more, till the thousand years should be fulfilled: and after that he must be loosed a little season. And I saw thrones, and they sat upon them, and judgment was given unto them: and I saw the souls of them that were beheaded for the witness of Jesus, and for the word of God, and which had not worshipped the beast, neither his image, neither had received his mark upon their foreheads, or in their hands; and they lived and reigned with Christ a thousand years. But the rest of the dead lived not again until the thousand years were finished. This is the first resurrection. Blessed and holy is he that hath part in the first resurrection: on such the second death hath no power, but they shall be priests of God and of Christ, and shall reign with him a thousand years. And when the thousand years are expired, Satan shall be loosed out of his prison, and shall go out to deceive the nations which are in the four quarters of the earth, Gog and Magog, to gather them together to battle: the number of whom is as the sand of the sea. And they went up on the breadth of the earth, and compassed the camp of the saints about, and the beloved city: and fire came down from God out of heaven, and devoured them. And the devil that deceived them was cast into the lake of fire and brimstone, where the beast and the false prophet are, and shall be tormented day and night for ever and ever (Revelation 20:1-10).

IN THE first chapters of this book we have thought together of what will happen when Jesus comes in the air, of what will happen in heaven after He comes in the air, of what will happen upon the earth after the Church is gone, and of what will happen when He comes in glory. In the last chapter we saw Him cast the Antichrist and the false prophet into the lake of fire and slay the armies of the world with the sword of His mouth. We saw Him judge the nations and restore Israel to a national standing.

Now we see the King of kings ready to mount the everlasting throne. He is going to set up His millennial kingdom which shall change all the earth. The word "millennium" is not mentioned in the Bible, but it simply means a period of a thousand years. There has been much misunderstanding about this period. It would have been better if Bible scholars had simply given the period the name "kingdom age" instead of "millennium."

Through the years men have dreamed of and sighed for a golden age. They have talked of the time when all men would be brothers and the earth would be filled with righteousness and peace. Many leaders today think they can bring in this kingdom age through education, through a league of nations, through better social conditions, or through other human agencies. Certainly these men are all wrong. It will take a superman to straighten out this old world. Human hands and human plans cannot do it. There is only One who can do it and the name of this Superman is the Lord Jesus Christ.

I. SATAN IS BOUND FOR A THOUSAND YEARS

An angel comes down from heaven with a key in his hand and a great chain upon his arm. He seizes Satan and binds him tightly for a thousand years. In verse 2 of our text four names are given to him . . . "the dragon, that old serpent . . . the Devil, and Satan." These names are expressive of all the evil which exists in him. Satan is put in a pit and locked up and a seal is placed upon his prison. You will remember that when Jesus died they put Him in a tomb, and the devil's gang demanded that a seal be placed upon this tomb. So Roman authorities did place a seal on the tomb of Jesus, but, with His mighty power, Jesus was able to burst this seal and come back to life again. Thank God, old Satan cannot break the seal that will be put upon the pit. When Christ puts him in it there will be no chance for him to escape. He must stay there until Christ releases him for a "little season."

You see, the millennium is to be a time of righteousness and peace. Therefore, it is absolutely necessary that Satan be removed from the earth. The postmillennialists and reformers who hope to bring about the millennium through their own power ignore the fact that you cannot have a millennium while the devil is still at work. They try to picture a golden age without getting rid of the devil and this can never be. Satan is behind every war, every evil custom, every sin and all opposition to the Gospel. He is too strong to be overcome by any human being or human method. Legislation will not move him. America passed a prohibition law but men still drank whisky because the devil still ruled in their hearts. The churches are victors over many things, but in spite of all their good work around the world the devil is still on the job. There is only One mightier than Satan . . . He is Christ, God's Son, and He must lock the devil up before we can have a millennium.

Now notice how easily He overcomes Satan. We read that He sent an angel to bind him. This was not Michael nor Gabriel, but one of the lesser angels. During the tribulation period the hosts of the earth and all the fallen angels fell before Satan and worshiped him. But now one of God's angels lays hold on him and ties him up for a thousand years.

In Isaiah 14:12-15 we read:

> How art thou fallen from heaven, O Lucifer, son of the morning! how art thou cut down to the ground, which didst weaken the nations! For thou hast said in thine heart, I will ascend into heaven, I will exalt my throne above the stars of God: I will sit also upon the mount of the congregation, in the sides of the north: I will ascend above the heights of the clouds; I will be like the most High. Yet thou shalt be brought down to hell, to the sides of the pit.

At last the roaring lion will be overcome by the Lion of the tribe of Judah. The Man with the bruised heel will crush the serpent's head. This will be a wonderful thing. Throughout the years Satan has tempted men, has made them fall and broken their hearts through sin. Now for one thousand years Satan will be locked up and Jesus will take the world over personally and run it in His own blessed way.

II. CHRIST SETS UP HIS MILLENNIAL THRONE

1. *Christ is spoken of in the Word as "Prophet," "Priest" and "King."* We have seen Him as Prophet and Priest, and now we see Him as King sitting upon the throne of David and reigning over all the world, a supreme and beneficent Sovereign. In Isaiah 9:6-7 we read:

> For unto us a child is born, unto us a son is given: and the government shall be upon his shoulder: and his name shall be called Wonderful, Counsellor, The mighty God, The everlasting Father, The Prince of Peace. Of the increase of his government and peace there shall be no end, upon the throne of David, and upon his kingdom, to order it, and to establish it with judgment and with justice from henceforth even for ever. The zeal of the Lord of hosts will perform this.

Also in Luke 1:30-33 we read:

> And the angel said unto her, Fear not, Mary: for thou hast found favour with God. And, behold, thou shalt con-

ceive in thy womb, and bring forth a son, and shalt call his name JESUS. He shall be great, and shall be called the Son of the Highest: and the Lord God shall give unto him the throne of his father David: and he shall reign over the house of Jacob for ever; and of his kingdom there shall be no end.

Both of these Scripture passages tell us that Jesus is going to be a King and that He is going to reign upon the throne of David. Well, He never has assumed that Kingship . . . He never has sat upon the throne of David. Therefore, these prophecies do not refer to His first coming. On that day, however, He will sit upon the throne and will be not only the King of the Jews, but the King of kings. The first time He came to the earth He was a poor peasant and had no place to lay His head. He was the poorest of the poor. On that day He will come in regal power and majesty and will become the Highest of the High. He came the first time as a Victim . . . He will come then as a Victor. Men put Him to death when He came the first time . . . He will rule over men when He comes the next time. Jerusalem will be the center of His kingdom in that day. It was at Jerusalem that they tried Him and beat Him and spat upon Him and killed Him . . . now He will reign over all the world from Jerusalem.

2. *Who will assist Him in this reign?* All the saints will be His assistants. He took them up when He came in the air . . . now He brings them back to reign in glory. They *lived* for Him upon the earth and now they will *reign* with Him upon the earth. Read Revelation 20:6: ". . . they shall be priests of God and of Christ, and shall reign with him a thousand years."

Through the years Christians have been persecuted and ridiculed and put to death. In that day they will be glorified with Him. Read Romans 8:18:

Simple Sermons on the Second Coming

> For I reckon that the sufferings of this present time are not worthy to be compared with the glory which shall be revealed in us.

Then read Luke 19:17:

> Well, thou good servant: because thou hast been faithful in a very little, have thou authority over ten cities.

These passages of Scripture tell us that the faithful will have a prominent place in the government of the world. Jesus and His saints will be one and He will share His glory with them. The world today looks down upon Christians . . . laughs and sneers at them . . . but in that day Jesus will give them a place higher even than the angels in heaven.

3. *The scope of His reign.* This reign will cover everything on the earth, under the earth and in the heavens. His exaltation is described in Philippians 2:9-11:

> Wherefore God also hath highly exalted him, and given him a name which is above every name: that at the name of Jesus every knee should bow, of things in heaven, and things in earth, and things under the earth; and that every tongue should confess that Jesus Christ is Lord, to the glory of God the Father.

This has not happened yet . . . all men have not yet bowed down to Jesus, but in that day everyone shall bow before Him.

The President does not personally superintend all the activities in our nation, and the king in any country cannot know personally everything that transpires in his kingdom. But Christ is Almighty and He sees everything and knows everything and has all power. His reign will touch every corner of the earth. He will know every person in the kingdom and He will govern every inch of space.

4. *The length of this reign.* It will last for a thousand years. This will be the interval between His coming in glory and the judgment of the Great White Throne. No

ruler ever ruled upon the earth for that length of time. One thousand is the perfect number and His reign will be the perfect reign.

5. *This reign will be the public honoring of God's Son.* Men dishonored and mistreated Him when He was here upon the earth, but in that day God will set Him up on high and give Him a name that is above every name and cause every knee to bow before Him.

Alvin York was a "hillbilly" from Tennessee. Very few people knew him, but one day he went overseas and came back a hero. General Pershing acclaimed him the greatest hero of World War One. When Alvin York came back to America his name was upon every lip. Great parades and wonderful banquets were held in his honor . . . rich gifts were bestowed upon him . . . his picture was in every magazine. This was a great change for the mountain lad from Tennessee, but it is nothing compared with the change in the treatment given to Christ. When He was upon the earth He became obedient unto death, even the death of the Cross. Cruel men seized Him and slew Him, but in that day God will highly exalt Him and cause the earth to bow before Him. They dishonored Him publicly before a few thousand in Jerusalem . . . then God will honor Him publicly before all the world.

6. *The prayers of the saints will be answered at last.* For many years God's people have prayed, "Thy kingdom come. Thy will be done in earth, as it is in heaven." In that day this prayer will be fully answered, for His kingdom will come and His will shall be done upon the earth.

Sometimes today we hear a man in a prayer say, "Lord, help us to bring in the kingdom." We cannot have a kingdom until the King comes back. We cannot set up a kingdom . . . He must do this. We hear other prayers which include this petition, "Lord, hasten the day when Thy kingdom shall come on earth." By this men mean the day when everybody will be a Christian and Christianity will be the force ruling the nations. This can never happen until Jesus comes back. We can have a great and perfect kingdom only when Christ comes and sits upon His throne and makes all things right.

III. LOOK AT THE CONDITIONS DURING THE MILLENNIUM

1. *The condition of the Jews.* They are God's timetable, and we must include them in every prophetic scheme.

In Genesis 13:14-15 we read:

> And the Lord said unto Abram, after that Lot was separated from him, Lift up now thine eyes, and look from the place where thou art northward, and southward, and eastward and westward: for all the land which thou seest, to thee will I give it, and to thy seed for ever.

The Jews have had deep sorrow. The land that God promised them has been taken away. They have been driven into every corner of the earth. However, in that day the promised land shall be theirs. Jerusalem will be restored in all of its glory. They will return to their own land and Jesus will rule in the midst of them. Here we see the wondrous grace of the Saviour. He came nineteen hundred years ago to the Jews as their Messiah and they rejected Him. "He came unto his own, and his own received him not." The Jews cried out, "Crucify him, crucify him." In that day He will gather them in His love and rule over them in grace and tenderness.

The great Temple will be rebuilt under Jesus Himself and the Shekinah glory of God will fill it. Palestine will be divided equally among the twelve tribes of Israel according to the forty-seventh chapter of Ezekiel. There are many other passages which describe the glory and blessedness which will come to the Jews during the millennial years. The nation which once rejected and crucified Christ will now turn to Him. God's chosen people will enjoy a season a thousand times more wonderful than any of those years spent under David and Solomon.

2. *The condition of the created earth.* When Adam fell, God put a curse upon the ground. Since then the earth has been in bondage. It is easy to grow weeds and briers without effort or planting, but it takes hard work to make the earth bring forth the things which man needs for food and clothing. We are told that when Christ returns creation will be delivered from her bondage. The desert will rejoice and blossom like a rose. There will be no famine nor drouths nor floods nor dust storms.

Even the animals will be changed. In the Garden of Eden the animals did not fight each other and they were not hostile to man, but sin brought a curse upon them as it did upon the whole earth. God meant His earth to be a veritable paradise, but it was ruined by man's sin. Ah, but when Jesus comes again He will make the world what God intended it to be! In Eden paradise was lost . . . when Jesus comes paradise will be regained. We are told about this in Isaiah 11:6-9:

> The wolf also shall dwell with the lamb, and the leopard shall lie down with the kid; and the calf and the young lion and the fatling together; and a little child shall lead them. And the cow and the bear shall feed; their young ones shall lie down together: and the lion shall eat straw like the ox. And the suckling child shall play on the hole of the asp, and the weaned child shall put his hand on the cockatrice' den. They shall not hurt nor destroy in all my holy mountain: for the earth shall be full of the knowledge of the Lord, as the waters cover the sea.

3. *Condition of the people of the earth.* Who are these people on the earth at this time? I am not speaking of the saints, for they shall be reigning with Him. These people will be those who are not slain in the battle of Armageddon, for some will have escaped death at that time. Many of their children will be living and will be here upon the earth.

Simple Sermons on the Second Coming

The Jewish remnant will be here. The Antichrist in the tribulation period slew some who did not follow him, but it is possible that they will be raised from the dead and will be here.

Now, all of these people shall be governed by Jesus with a rod of iron. It will not be a democracy, but a theocracy. He alone will be the ruler. Revelation 11:15 says:

> And the seventh angel sounded; and there were great voices in heaven, saying, The kingdoms of this world are become the kingdoms of our Lord, and of his Christ; and he shall reign for ever and ever.

The world has tried all types of government and all of them have failed. Monarchies, empires, republics, democracies and dictatorships have failed. Man has never found a perfect form of government. Now, the rule of Christ, even though it be a forced rule, will be a perfect one, a period in which there will be no graft and no political schemes.

There will be no sin upon the earth. Sin will still be in the hearts of men, but when it crops out Jesus will be in force and will put it down. The people on the earth will still be human and their hearts will still be wicked. If they were to be allowed absolute freedom the world would still witness murder and war and troubles, but He will rule with a rod of iron and will put all the evil down. Man will be forced to obey Christ in that period, but it will be a feigned obedience . . . an obedience not based on love and faith, but on fear.

There will be no wars, for the Prince of Peace will be ruling. This will be the first time since the flood that the earth has been free from the horrors of war. Today we talk about lasting peace but there will be no lasting peace upon the earth until the Prince of Peace reigns. Isaiah 2:4 reads:

> And he shall judge among the nations, and shall rebuke many people: and they shall beat their swords into plow-

shares, and their spears into pruninghooks: nation shall not lift up sword against nation, neither shall they learn war any more.

Today nations gather in peace conferences . . . they sign treaties . . . they make many plans. However, wars go on just the same and the world will always know the curse of war until Christ mounts the throne and causes war to cease from the earth. In 1914-1918 we fought a war to end all wars, but every year since then there has been a war somewhere in the world. Now we are engaged in the greatest war of all times, but in that millennial kingdom when the world is being run according to His great program there will be no wars nor rumors of wars.

In that period the world will have universal worship. We read in Zechariah 14:16:

> And it shall come to pass, that every one that is left of all the nations which came against Jerusalem shall even go up from year to year to worship the King, the Lord of hosts, and to keep the feast of tabernacles.

Today it is hard to get even a small percentage of the world's population to worship God . . . but in that day all nations will go up to worship Him.

IV. THE FINAL RESULTS OF THE MILLENNIUM

For one thousand years Christ will reign. He will place everything good in the world and keep everything bad out of the world. But men then will be even as they are today . . . their hearts will be sinful. In spite of the fact that they will be surrounded with all the blessings of God and none of the curse of Satan, their hearts will not have been changed.

Now Satan is loosed for a little season at the end of the thousand years. What does he do? He goes back to his old tricks of deceiving men, and man has one more opportunity to choose between Satan and Christ. What happens?

The nations flock to Satan's banner even as they do today. He gathers them all together and they go up to surround Jerusalem. They are going to make one more desperate effort to overcome Christ and His saints. Even then, however, some of the people on the earth will remain faithful to Christ, but the mass of them will follow Satan.

Can they have any success? No, of course not! "He that sitteth in the heavens shall laugh." God sends down fire from heaven and all of them are devoured by the flames. Satan is cast into the lake of fire. The Antichrist and the false prophet are there now and the unholy trinity is complete at last in the lake of fire. Satan's career is now ended . . . his work is over. He is in the place where he will be tormented day and night forever and ever. There will be no more sin. In the next chapter we shall see how Satan's followers are brought before the Great White Throne where they will receive eternal damnation and be cast into the lake of fire with him.

Here is one of the great Gospel truths which we have learned from the millennial study. All the external miracles, all the outside blessings, all the lovely environment . . . even if put there by Christ Himself . . . do not change man's heart and do not save him. This is eternally true, "Except a man be born again, he cannot see the kingdom of God." You may bring a pig into the house, give him a good bath and tie a red ribbon around his neck, but when the back door is opened he will dart out again and find his way to a mudhole. His nature has not been changed by these outside things. Man needs a change in nature and this change will be his only through the new birth. "Though your sins be as scarlet, they shall be as white as snow." "Him that cometh to me, I will in no wise cast out."

Where will you be during the millennium? Will you be reigning with Christ in glory, or will you be numbered among those who are hopelessly lost? It is up to you . . . now is the time for you to decide. An artist was talking to a class of art students. "When you paint a picture of the woods or forest," he said, "always paint a path leading out. If you do not have this path, anyone who looks at the picture will have a feeling of suffocation." In this book I have painted a picture for you of the terrors which are to come, but, thank God, the picture has a path leading out into the light. God Himself provided the Way. Jesus, His Son, has said, "I am the way." He is the only way to safety, to satisfaction and to salvation. He is the only way to hope, to happiness and to heaven. Will you not come to Jesus now and walk in that way?

6

WHAT WILL HAPPEN AT THE GREAT WHITE THRONE?

> And I saw a great white throne, and him that sat on it, from whose face the earth and the heaven fled away; and there was found no place for them. And I saw the dead, small and great, stand before God; and the books were opened: and another book was opened, which is the book of life: and the dead were judged out of those things which were written in the books, according to their works. And the sea gave up the dead which were in it; and death and hell delivered up the dead which were in them: and they were judged every man according to their works. And death and hell were cast into the lake of fire. This is the second death. And whosoever was not found written in the book of life was cast into the lake of fire (Revelation 20:11-15).

IN THE first chapter we noted what will happen when Jesus comes in the air; in the second chapter, what will happen in heaven after He comes in the air; in the third chapter, what will happen on the earth when the Church is gone, the manifestation and nature of the Antichrist and the period of tribulation. The fourth and fifth chapters covered the events of Christ's return in glory and the millennium. Now we are ready to study what will happen at the Great White Throne.

As the scene opens we have come to the end of the thousand years of peace, plenty and prosperity. The devil has been loosed for a season and we see the mass of the people following him and going with him against Christ and the saints. We then see the fire come out of heaven and kill all those who have followed Satan. The devil himself is then cast into the lake of fire and his career is over forever. Now in the next step we shall see the wicked dead being raised from their graves, and brought before the Great White Throne, where they shall be judged according to their works and cast into the lake of fire. Please remember that Christ is still reigning and that all power in heaven and in earth is His. Everything that happens at the Great White Throne will be under His supervision and power.

I. The Second Resurrection

If we are going to have a judgment we must bring up those who are to be judged. Let us see what God's Word says about the second resurrection.

> And many of them that sleep in the dust of the earth shall awake, some to everlasting life, and some to shame and everlasting contempt (Daniel 12:2).
>
> And shall come forth; they that have done good, unto the resurrection of life; and they that have done evil, unto the resurrection of damnation (John 5:29).
>
> The rest of the dead lived not again until the thousand years were finished . . . Blessed and holy is he that hath part in the first resurrection: on such the second death hath no power (Revelation 20:5-6).

These verses tell us clearly that there are two resurrections: the resurrection unto life which will be accomplished when Jesus comes in the air for His saints, and the resurrection unto death which will be accomplished when lost men will be called up before the Great White Throne. We are definitely and specifically told in these passages of a first resurrection and this clearly implies that there will be a second resurrection. As we think back over the previous chapters we remember that the first resurrection will take place when

Jesus comes in the air, for we read that "the dead in Christ shall rise first." This is the resurrection "out of the dead." Not all men will be raised at that time, but only those who have been saved through faith in Christ. The second resurrection will take place at the end of the millennium, for we read, "the rest of the dead lived not again until the thousand years were finished." At that time all dead lost men everywhere will be raised to appear before the Great White Throne. The graves and seas and deserts will give up their dead and there will not be one left anywhere.

II. THE GREAT WHITE THRONE

1. *We must distinguish this judgment from the other judgments.* There is first of all the judgment of the believers' sins. This happened on the Cross. We were guilty and someone had to pay the penalty of sin. Jesus did this for us at Calvary. Now we can say, "I am free from the judgment of sin because He took my condemnation on Himself there." Read Romans 8:1:

> There is therefore now no condemnation to them which are in Christ Jesus, who walk not after the flesh, but after the Spirit.

Read also John 5:24:

> Verily, verily, I say unto you He that heareth my word, and believeth on him that sent me, hath everlasting life, and shall not come into condemnation; but is passed from death unto life.

The next judgment is the one which takes place at the Judgment Seat of Christ. In Romans 14:10 we read: ". . . we shall all stand before the judgment seat of Christ." When He comes in the air He will set up this Judgment Seat and judge all Christians according to their works. They will then be rewarded according to their faithfulness and service and given crowns and rewards which they will enjoy throughout eternity.

Next is the judgment of the nations. When He comes in glory at the end of the tribulation period He will call all nations before Him, and He will judge them according to the treatment which they have given His Jewish brethren. Some of these nations will be cast out and some of them will be left to live through the kingdom period.

Now we come to the judgment of the Great White Throne. All lost men will be judged there and sent into everlasting punishment. Sometimes we hear a prayer in which these words occur: "Grant that we shall stand some day before the Great White Throne." Now this sounds good and we have in our mind a picture of a beautiful marble throne with Jesus sitting there to reward us. However, that is not a true picture of the Great White Throne. Christ will stand there as a Judge but not a single saved person will ever stand before the Great White Throne. Everyone who has been born again will be safe in Jesus and the Great White Throne will be a judgment of damnation for lost sinners.

2. *Where will the Great White Throne be located?* Apparently it will be set up in the upper heaven. We think of several heavens . . . there is the first heaven where we see the clouds drifting about, and there is the second heaven where we see the stars and the moon and the sun. Then there is the third heaven beyond this where God dwells. Paul tells us he was caught up into the third heaven one time, and he heard strange and wonderful things from the Lord. So it must be that the Great White Throne will be set up in that third heaven which God has made for His dwelling place.

The Bible tells us that when the Great White Throne is set up, heaven and earth will flee away and no place will be found for them. This means the earth which we know here and the atmospheric heaven which we see about us. The One upon the throne created the heavens and the earth and will cause them to obey the motion of His hand.

Why will He cause the earth to vanish? Because it is the scene of sin and sorrow . . . it has been stained by the Saviour's blood. Men hold on to the world now, but at that time the world will flee from them. Why does He cause the heavens to disappear? Because they have been polluted by Satan. He dwells in the heavens . . . he is "the prince of the power of the air." The heaven and the earth are not clean in God's sight and He will not let them remain.

This throne will not be a throne from which a King governs, but a throne from which a Judge pronounces doom. It is not a permanent throne, but it is set up for a specific purpose. Let us think of the three words connected with this throne. First there is the word *Great*. This throne is called great because of the greatness of the Judge and the solemnity of the occasion . . . because of the vastness of the scene and the eternal consequences involved. Christ offers you a great salvation now, but if you reject Him you will stand one day before the Great White Throne. Then there is the word *White*. This word corresponds to the character of the Judge . . . the whiteness tells us of His purity and holiness. Imagine the contrast here . . . the sinners who face Him will be black with the sin of rejection, and He will be white as the light. A lost man will not be able to stand for one second in that Presence. Now we come to the word *Throne*. This means unlimited majesty and authority.

3. *Who will be judged at the Great White Throne?* Not all men who have lived will be judged, but only lost men . . . unbelievers in Christ. John said, "I saw the dead, small and great, stand before God." The saved ones will not be before Him, but all lost people of all ages will stand before this throne. Death holds the bodies of the unsaved dead and the text tells us that death and hades will give up all of their dead at this time. The bodies and spirits of the unsaved will then be joined together and automatically brought before the Great White Throne.

Now they know how they have rejected Christ, they know the penalty of rejection and they try to escape. We read in Revelation 6:15-17:

> And the kings of the earth, and the great men, and the rich men, and the chief captains, and the mighty men, and every bondman, and every free man, hid themselves in the dens and in the rocks of the mountains; and said to the mountains and rocks, Fall on us, and hide us from the face of him that sitteth on the throne, and from the wrath of the Lamb: for the great day of his wrath is come; and who shall be able to stand?

The text says first that the small and great will stand before God. Wealth and power will not save you from appearing at the Great White Throne. Neither will poverty save you. Some murderers will be there . . . not because they murdered, but because they rejected Christ. Some good men who helped the poor and lived well for their families and communities will be there, simply because they rejected Jesus Christ. All distinctions will be swept away. The Judge will be no respecter of persons. The proud and the mighty as well as the nobodies will be there to furnish fuel for the lake of fire.

This will be a final judgment and from its verdicts there will be no appeal. Remember that if you have lived without Christ you will some day appear before the Great White Throne and there will be no chance for you. You will not even speak . . . you will know that you are guilty and will bow your head to receive a just and righteous condemnation. We read that "death and hell were cast into the lake of fire." These are two of the awful things brought into the world by sin. In that day God will have no more use for them and will throw them into the lake of fire along with "the devil that deceived them . . . [and] the beast and the false prophet."

4. *Who will be the Judge at the Great White Throne?* God has ordained a judge for this occasion. Read Acts 17:31:

> . . . he [God] hath appointed a day, in the which he will judge the world in righteousness by that man whom he hath ordained, whereof he hath given assurance unto all men, in that he hath raised him from the dead.

Jesus is the One whom God raised . . . Jesus will be the Judge. He will settle all accounts at that time. He has already dealt with Satan and cast him into the lake of fire, and now He will deal with all those who followed Satan in life.

Jesus stood before Pilate and the creature judged the Creator. Now the creatures will stand before the Creator and receive the ratification of their damnation. In Pilate's hall Jesus stood speechless . . . at the Great White Throne men will be speechless. He once stood condemned before a throne of this world . . . in that day He will sit upon a throne and judge all those who condemned Him. As men look into the face of that Judge they will remember that His face was once spat upon and beaten and stained with blood. In that day His face will be so majestic that sinners will want to flee from the sight of it. He will not judge alone but He will be assisted by all of the saints. He will share all of His glory and responsibility with them. When we see Him and know what He really is and remember those who rejected Him, we will say "Amen" to their condemnation, even though they be our loved ones, for in that day we will see the rightness of everything which He does.

How terrible it is for a man to go through life rejecting Christ, and then one day to come face to face with the unapproachable Light, unforgiven and doomed forever. Christ is filled with mercy toward you today, and you can come to Him and be saved, but in that day mercy will have passed and the time of condemnation will be at hand.

The story is told of a judge who saved a man's life. Later on this man committed a crime and was brought before this particular judge to be sentenced. Recognizing the judge, the man cried out: "Don't you remember me,

Judge? I am the man whom you saved! Have mercy on me now." The judge grimly replied, "I remember you, but things are different now . . . I was your saviour then, but I am your judge now." Jesus is our Saviour now . . . He offers to save all those who come unto Him. If you do not come to Him now, in that day He will be your Judge.

5. *The purpose of the Great White Throne judgment.* The purpose of the judgment will not be to decide whether a man is saved or lost . . . that is decided here upon the earth. The lost man is as good as damned here upon the earth. "He that believeth not is condemned already." You go into a prison and walk down death row and look at a man in a certain cell. The warden says to you, "This man is facing death. He is to be electrocuted next Tuesday." When you look at a man who is rejecting Jesus Christ, you are looking at a man whom God says is condemned already . . . one who is facing eternal death which will be meted out to him at the Great White Throne. The judgment at that time will be simply a just confirmation of the sinner's death sentence. It will not be God's fault, but will come about because of the hardness of the man's heart.

There will be no more sin after this judgment. In God's new creation sin is forever excluded. Satan, the author of sin, will be cast into the lake of fire. All sinners will be there with him and God's people will be made perfect . . . they will be like unto Jesus. So a wondrous thing will come to pass . . . there will be no more sin anywhere.

Degrees of punishment will be decided upon at the Great White Throne. At that time it will be "more tolerable" for some people than for others. As there are degrees of rewards for those who are saved, so will there be degrees of punishment for those who are lost.

Here are the dictators of the world who have shed the innocent blood of millions and brought great affliction upon the human race, and here is a good man who has lived a clean moral life, but who was not a Christian. Both of these shall be lost and cast into the lake of fire, but surely the ones whose sins were more grievous will suffer more intensely, and this will be right.

A man dies and his life is over, but the works of that man live on. In that day all the facts will be in and men will be judged not only by what they did in life, but by their influence which lived after them. For example, a man writes a book which leads men away from God. This book lives on and does its damaging work after the man is dead. At that day he will be punished according to all of his works whether they were accomplished in his lifetime or not. For another example, here is a man who leads a younger man into sin. The older man soon dies, but the sinful acts which he prompted still live on in the younger man. At the Great White Throne all evil will be ended and full punishment will be determined for all sinners.

6. *The books to be used at the Great White Throne.* We need to make a distinction here. First, there is the Lamb's book of life. This is Christ's record of His saved ones. The minute you are saved your name is written in that book. In Luke 10:20 Jesus told His disciples to rejoice because their names were written in heaven.

Then there is the book of records. This book will contain all the deeds and thoughts of the unsaved, and at the Great White Throne they will be judged according to the records of this book. You may forget some of your sins, but God is writing all the time and the record will be there in His book.

The great railroads of our country have their car departments which employ thousands of men. These men can tell you at any time where every car belonging to their system is located. They can tell you whether it is part of a train or sitting on a sidetrack . . . whether it is on their own tracks or upon the tracks of another railroad system. They can tell you its number, size, age, state of repair, and whether it is loaded or empty. I tell you that if a railroad company can keep such records, God can keep a record of all you do and say. There are millions of men in the service of our country, but the adjutant general's office in Washington can tell you the serial number of every man, where he is, his rank, his age, the name of his dependents and all about him. If man can keep such records, God can keep even greater records. A great symphony orchestra plays for one hour and the music is recorded on a record of wax. In the years to come that record, placed upon a special machine, will give you every tone and every note which the orchestra played in that one hour. In like manner God has made a record of every life and that record will face sinners at the Great White Throne.

When detectives want to catch a criminal they sometimes hide a dictaphone in a room and from the conversation recorded they learn the plot of the crime. When the criminal is captured the record is played back to him. There is no use of his denying the plot, for there is the record of his misdeeds. In that day of the Great White Throne the records of life will confront unbelievers and there will be no use of their denying their sins. It will all be there before them. So this judgment will not be a trial as we think of trials, but will be a great public manifestation of the facts which have already been settled and recorded.

Then there is the book of life. The names of all people who have ever been born will be in this book, but the names of the unsaved will be blotted out. This will leave only the names of the saved ones, and this will make the book identical with the Lamb's book of life. In Revelation 3:5 Christ promises that the believer's name will never be blotted out of the book of life. This indicates that some names will be blotted out. Since the names of the saved *cannot* be blotted out, it remains that the names of the lost ones *will* be blotted out. At the Great White Throne the Judge will look for the names of the unsaved in the book of life. Since their names will not be there, this will be another confirmation of a righteous judgment.

At the Great White Throne some men will probably make a vain plea. They will say, "We did thus and so . . . we gave our money . . . we performed many good deeds." Then the Judge will look into the book and their names will not be there. Some will say, "My mother was a Christian and my father was a godly man." The Judge will reply, "But your name is not written in the book of life." You may have many good things in the record book, but if your name is not written in the great book of life, you will be lost forever. You may be trying to get by in life by doing a few good things along the way. You are helpful and kind and considerate of others. These things make you feel good and they ease your conscience, but there is no hope for you if your name is not written in the book of life.

7. *The sentence of the Great White Throne judgment.* "Whosoever was not found written in the book of life was cast into the lake of fire." A woman said to me some time ago, "I don't believe that these things will happen." Well, shall we go by our own fancies or by the plain teachings of the Scriptures? The place of punishment for sinners is given various names in the Bible. We read about the lake of fire, the second death, outer darkness, and the place of wailing and gnashing of teeth. If there is no such place of punishment, why does the Bible say so much about it? We are told in Revelation 20:10 that "the devil . . . was cast into the lake of fire . . . and shall be tormented day and night for ever and ever." If you are lost you will be sent to the same place and the same thing will happen to you. You will suffer day and night forever and ever. I do not say this . . . God said it. Will you call Him a liar? We talk today about doomsday . . . this will be the day of doom for sinners. "[They] shall have their part in the lake

which burneth with fire and brimstone." Now I have a word for the Christian. You will not be judged at the Great White Throne, but the thought of that awful judgment should solemnize you and should make you want to win the lost to Christ so they may be kept from the Great White Throne and all of its consequences. That is my task also . . . that is why I preach Christ over and over and over again.

III. How Can You Escape Appearing Before the Great White Throne?

Simply by coming to Jesus now. He will save you and keep you, and when He comes in the air He will take you up to be with Him forever. If you refuse to come to Him, He will raise you up before the Great White Throne and the hand which was pierced for you on the Cross will be lifted up and will point your way down and down and down forever. You will go down into the lake of fire where with the devil you will be tormented day and night forever and ever. You followed him upon the earth and then you will have to stay with him throughout all eternity.

Let us listen to the advice of an infidel whose name was Ethan Allen. He was a famous New England soldier. He spoke out everywhere against religion. One day his daughter lay dying, and called him to her bedside. She said to him: "Daddy, I am going to die. Mother says that there is a Christ and a hereafter. You scoff at such things. I am dying now, and I must make my final decision in this minute. Which one of you shall I believe? Shall I accept my mother's Christ or your infidelity?" The great soldier's frame shook with sobs and he cried out: "My darling, it would be better for you to die in your mother's faith and not in my unbelief. Give your heart to Jesus." This is good advice. Do not go on any longer in sin and unbelief. Come to Jesus now, for only through Him will you find a way to escape the damnation of the Great White Throne.

7

WHAT WILL HAPPEN WHEN THE WORLD IS NO MORE?

> And I saw a new heaven and a new earth: for the first heaven and the first earth were passed away; and there was no more sea. And I John saw the holy city, new Jerusalem, coming down from God out of heaven, prepared as a bride adorned for her husband. And I heard a great voice out of heaven saying, Behold, the tabernacle of God is with men, and he will dwell with them, and they shall be his people, and God himself shall be with them, and be their God. And God shall wipe away all tears from their eyes; and there shall be no more death, neither sorrow, nor crying, neither shall there be any more pain: for the former things are passed away (Revelation 21:1-4). (Read the entire chapter.)

THIS IS the last chapter in our book. We have tried to take, in proper order, all of the events connected with our Lord's Second Coming. We have seen Him come in the air and take up His saints. We have seen Him in heaven rewarding His saints at the Judgment Seat, and sitting with them at the Marriage Supper of the Lamb. We have looked upon the earth after the Church has been taken away. We have seen Jesus coming in glory, we have studied the millennial period and we have witnessed the judgment of the Great White Throne. Now we come to our closing chapter, "What Will Happen When the World Is No More?"

Some years ago when I was finishing my studies at Wake

Forest College, I was called to the pastorate of the First Baptist Church of Hendersonville, North Carolina. After this call had been accepted I went to Hendersonville and looked for a house in which to live during my pastorate there. After I had found a suitable place, I called my wife on the long distance telephone and told her all about this house. Then when I had returned to Wake Forest I described the house in detail, and drew a plan of the rooms for her, so that she might know something about our future home. In like manner, I believe that every true Christian has the desire to know something about his future heavenly home. Some will say, "But we know nothing about heaven . . . Jesus is the only One who has ever come back from that place." Yes, and He is the One who tells us about it. John was banished to the Isle of Patmos, and since Jesus wanted to give us a message about heaven and future events, He pinned the curtain of eternity back and permitted John to look into heaven. Surely as this great old man of God began to pen his picture of the heavenly city, he must have felt that language was inadequate to describe the glories of that lovely place.

A woman said to one of our Bible teachers lately, "Why doesn't the Bible tell us more about heaven?" And the teacher replied, "If God told us more about heaven we would be so anxious to go there that we would not do our work here as it ought to be done." Paul tells us that on one occasion he was taken into the third heaven. The vision which he had there was so wonderful that God almost had to tie him down upon the earth to keep him here. Paul said at one time that it is far better "to depart, and to be with Christ."

John had just seen all of the glories of heaven. He knew that soon Jesus would be coming back and that His coming would be a prelude to our entrance into heaven. And as the old saint told of the glories that awaited him, his heart overflowed and he cried out, "Even so, come, Lord Jesus."

After the Great White Throne judgment, Satan is gone and sinners are with him in the lake of fire. Now comes the perfect age of eternity. Every purpose of God for man will now find its fulfillment.

I. THE PRESENT HEAVEN AND EARTH WILL PASS AWAY

Bible scholars are divided upon this question. Some of them say that heaven and earth will not be destroyed, but will simply be cleansed and purified. Then they say that this earth will be the future home of God and His saints. Other scholars say that heaven and earth will actually be destroyed and will vanish. We cannot be dogmatic about this, but from my studies of related Scripture passages and the comments of great Bible scholars, I have come to believe that heaven and earth will really pass away and that a new heaven and earth will take their place. This is what we are told in Revelation 21:1:

> And I saw a new heaven and a new earth: for the first heaven and the first earth were passed away.

There is an organ in the corner of our church. Suppose I tell you that this organ is going to be taken away this week and replaced with a new one. Then on next Sunday when you come to church I say to you, "The old organ is gone now and we have a new one in its place." Would you look for a fresh coat of paint on the old organ? Would you listen to determine whether the old organ had been tuned up? No, you would expect to see a new organ. Well, our Scripture verse says that this old heaven and earth will pass away and that they will be replaced by a new heaven and a new earth. In II Peter 3:10 we read:

> But the day of the Lord will come as a thief in the night; in the which the heavens shall pass away with a great noise, and the elements shall melt with fervent heat, the earth also and the works that are therein shall be burned up.

Isaiah 65:17 declares:

> For, behold, I create new heavens and a new earth: and the former shall not be remembered, nor come into mind.

When God says that He will "create," what does He mean? He means that He is going to call into existence something which did not previously exist. In Genesis 1:1 we read: "In the beginning God created the heaven and the earth." He made the earth and sun and moon and stars. He created the animals, growing things and man. He had nothing with which to begin. He simply spoke and these things came into existence. Now, you can build a table or make a cake, but you must use pre-existent materials. However, when God creates He makes something out of nothing, so I say that He will create a new heaven and a new earth. God will not use the old heaven and the old earth. These are passed away . . . they will be utterly destroyed. Then He will create an absolutely new heaven and new earth.

In the Bible the term "creation" is used one hundred and twenty times, and each time it is used it means the origin of things and not the cleansing or the change of some old thing. John saw a new heaven and a new earth. Then he heard a voice out of heaven saying, "Behold, I make all things new." Everything will be a new creation from the great hand of the Father.

Jesus said, "Heaven and earth shall pass away, but my words shall not pass away." Both this passage and the one in Revelation 21 refer to the heaven and earth which we can see and not the abode of God Himself, which is the third heaven. So our text must be telling us that all of the earth which we see here and all of the heavens which stand between us and God will be absolutely destroyed at that time.

That new creation will be so different that there will be no need of sun nor moon nor stars. The place where these things are located today will be gone . . . even the laws of nature will pass away. You will remember after the Resurrection how Jesus could transcend space and walk through closed doors. He was showing them that He belonged to a realm where all things were new. In Revelation 21:4 we read: "The former things are passed away." This means heaven and earth and all the things in them. Therefore, I believe that the earth and all things in it will be destroyed, that the heavens which we see and all things in them will also be utterly destroyed, and that then God will create a new heaven and a new earth and will place them just where He wants them. He can do all this in a second of time.

Man's history is now over and God's new order has begun. Man made a failure of this world order and only God could create and continue a perfect state. The dark day is over and the sun has risen to shine forever. There will be no weeping for this old earth as it passes away. It was here that sin held sway . . . it was here that disease and death came . . . it was here that sorrows and sadness broke our hearts . . . it was here that the hillsides and valleys were soaked with the blood of our loved ones who fought in futile wars. It was here that Christ, the Lamb, was crucified. This old world has been cursed and we shall be glad to see it go.

II. THE NEW JERUSALEM

John saw the new heaven and the new earth and then, in his vision, an angel led him to a place from which he saw a great city, the New Jerusalem, coming down out of heaven. The foundations of this city are to rest upon the new earth and this New Jerusalem will be our heavenly home. Now, why is this city called the New Jerusalem, instead of New York or some other name? Well, Jerusalem is the city which He loved above all others. It will be God's capital city and all the saints will dwell in it with Him. Previously, God has been in heaven and man has been upon the earth.

In the New Jerusalem the situation will be changed. John heard a "voice out of heaven saying, Behold, the tabernacle of God is with men and he will dwell with them, and they shall be his people, and God himself shall be with them, and be their God."

Now let us see what the Bible says of this New Jerusalem.

1. *It will be a real city . . . a literal city.* The Bible describes the city literally and tells us that it is made of real material. Why did God tell us of the gold and the pearls and the other things in the city if they were not made of real material? Why did He give us the dimensions of the city if it were not real? You cannot measure a city that is not real. He told us of the inhabitants of this city, but there could be no one dwelling in it if it were not a real city.

In Hebrews 11:10 we read that ". . . he [Abraham] looked for a city which hath foundations, whose builder and maker is God." The old earth which has now passed away was a real place and the New Jerusalem which comes down to rest upon the earth is a real city. Jesus said, "I go to prepare a place for you" . . . not simply a condition or a state of being, but a place. The New Jerusalem is a literal place . . . a wonderful place.

2. *It will be a city sent down from heaven.* He "shewed me that great city, the holy Jerusalem, descending out of heaven from God." Everything that God sends down out of heaven is infinitely good. Nineteen hundred years ago He sent Jesus down as His best Gift, and all the world has been blessed by that Gift. When He brings heaven down to us we know that again He will be bringing His best. A king once gave a diamond to one of his friends, and the friend said, "Sir, this is too great a gift for me to receive." But the king answered, "It is not too great a gift for a king to give." In like manner heaven is too much for us

and we do not deserve it, but it is not too much for God to give. It is just like Him to present us with such a gift.

3. *It will be a vast city.* In Revelation 21:15 John tells us that the angel measured the city, the gates and the walls. He found it to be a great city lying foursquare. It has been figured that the New Jerusalem will be fifteen hundred miles long, fifteen hundred miles wide and fifteen hundred miles high. Surely it is a city of great magnitude. Some of the cities of the world are not beautiful, but the New Jerusalem is a city of perfect symmetry and perfect beauty, laid out by the hand of the great Architect.

Today traveling conditions are quite difficult. Trains and buses and planes are crowded. A trip of fifteen hundred miles is an ordeal. But in the New Jerusalem, when you want to go from one side of the city to another, you can cover the fifteen hundred miles in a fraction of a second. You will have a glorified body which transcends space and devours distance.

4. *It will be the city of God's home.* The Bible refers often to God's throne. We have thought of Him as dwelling in the thick clouds far away from our little lives. We think of Him in a high and mighty position, but we have never seen Him at home. You do not really know anyone until you see him at home. Now, in the New Jerusalem God will be at home and we will be with Him and we will know Him as He is.

Jesus had no home while He was on earth. He said that the birds of the air had nests and the foxes had holes, but that He had no place to lay His head. Ah, but in the New Jerusalem He will have a wonderful home at last!

5. *It will be a city of God's government.* Heretofore in the judgments, in the millennium and in the prophetic sermons, Christ has been the ruling figure and God has been in the background. But now Christ has finished His work,

God will appear and Christ will deliver everything up to Him. We read in I Corinthians 15:24:

> Then cometh the end, when he shall have delivered up the kingdom to God, even the Father; when he shall have put down all rule and all authority and power.

Revelation 22:3 tells us:

> But the throne of God and of the Lamb shall be in it.

After Christ delivers up the kingdom unto His Father, God will elevate the Son to His own throne, and will reign with Him. The Holy Spirit is the other person of the Trinity and cannot be separated from the Godhead. Evidently He will also be there in His respective position and doing His respective work. In Genesis the three of them together said, "Let us make man in our own image." Now they will together enjoy heaven with man after he has been redeemed.

6. *It will be a city of saints.* In Revelation 21:7 we read:

> He that overcometh shall inherit all things.

I John 5:5 declares:

> Who is he that overcometh the world, but he that believeth that Jesus is the Son of God?

The city will be inhabited by the saints of God . . . the believers in Christ. There is no mention made here of the angels, but surely they will be there, too. However, I believe that the redeemed saints will have a place higher in heaven than the angels.

In Revelation 22:4 we read:

> His name shall be in their foreheads.

His name reveals to us the nature and character of God. That name will be in our foreheads for every one to see and each of us will perfectly and publicly reflect the character of God.

7. *It will be a city of blessed fellowship.* God's eternal plan was to be with man and to enjoy fellowship with him. Satan's eternal purpose was to separate man and God. But now Satan's day is over and man and God are together forever. Read Revelation 21:3:

> And I heard a great voice out of heaven saying, Behold, the tabernacle of God is with men, and he will dwell with them, and they shall be his people, and God himself shall be with them, and be their God.

Revelation 3:4 tells us:

> . . . and they shall walk with me in white: for they are worthy.

In the Garden of Eden God walked with man and had fellowship with him. Sin soon entered into the garden and man and God were separated and their fellowship broken up. But never again will Satan be able to break up this wonderful fellowship. As you look through the Bible you see God marching against all obstacles, over every mountain, through every valley, even through Gethsemane and Calvary, in order that finally He could be at home with man. He will wipe away all of our tears and cause us to forget every bad thing, and man will enjoy God forever.

We shall have blessed fellowship with others also. The words of the hymn are true:

> *Friends will be there I have loved long ago,*
> *Joy like a river around me will flow.*

Friendships are broken here, but not in heaven. In the vocabulary of God there is no such word as "good-bye" . . . those who love Him never part for the last time.

8. *It will be a prepared city.* We read in John 14:2: "I go to prepare a place for you," and in Revelation 21:2: "I . . . saw the holy city, new Jerusalem, coming down from God out of heaven, prepared as a bride adorned for her husband." A bride comes to the altar clean and spotless

and happy. She has been prepared. Likewise the New Jerusalem will be a prepared city.

When a man builds a city he gathers many materials from many places. God uses many materials in building the New Jerusalem. He uses the most expensive materials which exist . . . gold, pearls and precious stones. One of the stones mentioned is a sardius. The color of this stone is bright red and symbolizes the blood of Christ. When we enter the New Jerusalem we will probably learn that every precious stone used there is significant of some great spiritual truth.

We are told that "the street of the city was pure gold." Gold stands for divine righteousness. With our sins gone forever, we shall walk in that city in a state of perfect righteousness. Men will do anything in this world for gold . . . they will rob and cheat and murder in order to get it. Thank God, in heaven at last gold will be under our feet and we shall worship it no longer.

9. *It will be a city of divine Light.* Revelation 22:5 tells us:

> And there shall be no night there; and they need no candle, neither light of the sun; for the Lord God giveth them light.

It is said that Niagara Falls, New York, is the most brilliantly lighted city in all the world. But no city of this world can compare with the New Jerusalem, which will be lighted by God's great glory. We shall not then be forced to depend upon nature's light, for the sun and the moon and the stars will be gone. All the light we need will come from God, and His glory will fill the city.

"There shall be no night there." Night is a symbol of evil. Most crimes are committed during the night hours. Those who are sick watch for the morning. "Weeping may endure for a night, but joy cometh in the morning." There will be no night in that wonderful city . . . all of us will be blessed by the divine Light forever. The divine Light there is in contrast to the present world of darkness . . . spiritual darkness and physical darkness fill the world. Only one half of this world can be light at one time, but then His light will fill all of heaven at all times. The city of the saints can be contrasted to the place of lost souls. They will be in outer darkness while the saved will be living in a city of divine Light.

10. *It will be a walled city.* Read Revelation 21:12:

> [The city] had a wall great and high, and had twelve gates, and at the gates twelve angels, and names written thereon, which are the names of the twelve tribes of the children of Israel.

Now note that each of these gates has the name of one of the tribes of Israel. Also note the twelve foundations of the city as given in verse 14. Here we are told that these foundation stones bear the names of the apostles of the Lamb. You see, this is a memorial wall covering both the Old Testament and the New Testament times, and constantly reminding us of the works of Old Testament Israel and the New Testament Church.

The wall is made of jasper. God is rich and He does not have to use common stone or common bricks or marble. He uses precious stones in building that great wall. The Chinese wall was once thought to be one of the wonders of the world, but it has been in ruins for many years. God's wall will last forever as a symbol of His protection and as a picture of the manner in which His love surrounds us.

11. *It will be a city with a new Temple.* John tells us in Revelation 21:22:

> And I saw no temple therein: for the Lord God Almighty and the Lamb are the temple of it.

The purpose of a temple is to furnish a place for the worship of God. Yet we do not see God in these temples, and so they are merely shadows of the great Temple which is to come. In the New Jerusalem we will really worship Him for He is the Temple. We shall not worship an unseen Being, but shall look into His dear face. All of our worship will center in the throne where He is.

Down here our church services may not always be joyful and worshipful, but up there they will always be full of great joy and great blessing. The other day a man said to me, "I look forward to attending every service." Surely that will be our true attitude in that day. In the millennium the nations come once each year to worship the King . . . in the New Jerusalem every act will be one of worship and every day we shall learn something new about Jesus. Every day we shall be expressing new gratitude to Him as we learn how much He has meant to us and how much it does mean for us to be there with Him.

12. *It will be a city of one language.* In Zephaniah 3:9 we learn:

> For then will I turn to the people a pure language, that they may all call upon the name of the Lord, to serve him with one consent.

At the tower of Babel God brought about a confusion of tongues. This was another result of sin. Today there are hundreds of languages and dialects in the world, but in that day we shall speak only one language, and every sentence will be filled with praise to the Lamb who was slain from the foundation of the world.

13. *It will be a city of service.* Revelation 22:3 tells us:

> And his servants shall serve him.

We shall not sit through eternity playing our harps and doing nothing. We shall go home and lay our sheaves at His feet and He will then make us able to render perfect service. We shall never be tired and never discouraged. We shall enjoy every minute of our service.

14. *It will be a city where there will be no more curse.* Sin brought a curse upon the earth and upon mankind, but there will be no more sin and no more curse in the New Jerusalem. Satan will be banished and sin will be forever absent. There will be no tragedies and we shall never hear of murder, war and suicides. The present Jerusalem is unholy but the New Jerusalem will be a holy city.

God built the first Garden of Eden and sin came into this garden and ruined everything. All things that grew in the garden withered and died. This was true, not only of the flowers of the field, but of the man whom God had made. However, in that day the curse will be removed, not only from man, but even from plant life and they shall have eternal life.

Revelation 21:27 tells us:

> And there shall in no wise enter into it any thing that defileth.

The things which sin brought on will never be able to get into heaven. No wonder it is such a marvelous city.

There will be no more tears. Tears flow freely here . . . all of us shed them at times. Up there they will be wiped away by the loving hand of our Heavenly Father. There will be no more sorrow there. Who sees more sorrow than a busy pastor? He sees God's people with their hearts breaking and their tears flowing, but, thank God, sorrow can never enter into the New Jerusalem. There will be no more pain. Pain is a tragic thing . . . it comes to the young and the old, to the rich and the poor, the good and the bad. However, none of it can ever come there and we shall never have to worry about sickness, disease, pestilence or broken limbs.

Now look at the contrast between this land and the land of the lost. Those in the lake of fire are "tormented day and night for ever and ever." In heaven there is no pain.

We know what pain is here, but it will be a million times worse in hell with no relief in sight.

You can take your choice now . . . it is Christ or sin, heaven or hell, torment or bliss.

There will be no more sea. This was a comfort to John's heart. While he was on the Isle of Patmos the sea separated him from his loved ones. In heaven there will be nothing to separate us from our loved ones. The Lord's people will be together forever. Here we need the sea to equalize the temperature. The earth, sky and sea combine to furnish us an atmosphere in which we can live in health. But there, in our glorified bodies which will be adjusted to everything, there will be no more need of the sea. Then, again, the sea is a type of restlessness and in that day there will be no more restlessness for individuals or for nations.

There will be no more death. Death knocks at our doors and we say, "Go away, death, I am not ready!" We bolt the doors against death, but death knocks down the door and comes in just the same. In that great city there will be no more death and no graves on the hillsides of glory. In Revelation 20:14 we read that death is cast into the lake of fire. It is the last enemy that shall be destroyed. It has a sting here . . . it crushes here . . . it breaks hearts here . . . but, thank God, it will never enter into the New Jerusalem.

15. *It will be an eternal city.* Hebrews 13:14 reads:

> For here we have no continuing city, but we seek one to come.

The great cities of the world will not continue . . . they will soon perish in the dust. But, thank God, the New Jerusalem will last forever. Revelation 22:5 tells us that "they shall reign for ever and ever." Yes, it will be an eternal city in which God's people will dwell.

16. *It will be a city where we shall see His face.* If heaven is simply a great city with streets of gold, gates of pearl, precious stones and great distances, it will not be

enough. It would not be worth the struggle. But it is more than all of this . . . it is a place where we shall see Jesus. If we could not see Him, it would not be heaven for us. There are others whom we shall long to see, but first of all we want to see our Saviour.

> *Oh, the dear ones in glory,*
> *How they beckon me to come,*
> *And our parting at the river I recall;*
> *To the sweet vales of Eden*
> *They will sing my welcome home;*
> *But I long to meet my Saviour first of all.*

Then we shall understand all things. We shall forget the hard struggle of life when we see His face. We shall know that everything that ever happened to us was simply leading to that great hour and that great privilege.

> *Face to face with Christ my Saviour,*
> *Face to face — what will it be;*
> *When with rapture I behold Him,*
> *Jesus Christ who died for me?*

There will be only one word to express our feeling. David used it when he said, "I shall be satisfied, when I awake, with thy likeness." Yes, when we see Him and know that we are going to dwell with Him throughout eternity we shall be forever and fully satisfied.

You can have a part in this glory and you can enjoy these eternal blessings, all because there was One who made it possible by His death on Calvary's Cross. Believe in Him . . . come to Him. He will receive you and give you a place in heaven.

In Revelation 21:8 we are told about those who will not be there:

> But the fearful, and unbelieving, and the abominable, and murderers, and whoremongers, and sorcerers, and idolaters, and all liars, shall have their part in the lake which burneth with fire and brimstone: which is the second death.

Now you see what becomes of sinners. Does someone say, "I am not a Christian, but I am surely not included in that list"? Yes, you are included in this list because the verse tells us that all unbelievers shall be lost. The message for us is very plain: Believe on Him and heaven will be your portion . . . live without Him and you will be cast into the lake of fire.

In Vienna, Austria, there is a famous chapel where the royal members of the Hapsburg family have been buried for the past five hundred years. When a member of the family dies he is taken to this chapel where an impressive ceremony takes place. The chaplain performs the funeral service in the palace, then leads the procession down toward the chapel for the burial. Upon arriving at the chapel the chaplain knocks upon the door. The prior of the chapel comes to the door, but does not open it. Instead he cries out, "Who is there?"

When the Emperor Franz Josef was being buried, the chaplain answered, "I ask admittance for the body of Franz Josef, Emperor of Austria, King of Hungary, King of the Romans, King of Illyria." The prior spoke back through the little wicket, "I know no Franz Josef, Emperor of Austria, King of Hungary, King of the Romans, King of Illyria." Once more the chaplain knocked. Again he gave the titles of the great man, and again he received the same answer from the prior. The chaplain hesitated a minute, then knocked again and said, "I ask admission for Franz Josef, a poor sinner." The prior immediately swung open the door and said, "Enter Franz Josef, poor sinner."

My friend, you may come with all of your good works and you may boast of the many good deeds you have done, but you will not get into the gates of heaven, even though there be twelve of them. But come to Jesus, your Saviour . . . come as a poor sinner. He will take you into His heart at once and some day you will enter the New Jerusalem with Him, and never, never be forced to leave it.